The **Desire Code**

7 Keys to fulfill your wishes for success, wealth and happiness

The **Desire Code**
7 Keys to fulfill your wishes for success, wealth and happiness

Pierre Franckh
Munich • London
Copyright © 2015 Pierre Franckh

German Copyright © 2009 by KOHA-Verlag GmbH Burgrain
Originally published in Germany under the title:
Erfolgreich Wünschen, 7 Regeln wie Träume wahr werden
by KOHA-Verlag

The **Desire Code**
7 Keys to fulfill your wishes for success, wealth and happiness

Project Management by Michaela Merten
Translated by Katerina Tepla
Edited by Lorna Smeadman and Paul Parry
Cover Design by Renaud Defrancesco

First U.S: edition published by
Pierre Franckh & Michaela Merten,
81545 Munich, Germany

ISBN 978-3-946547-33-4

Also available as an

www.pierre-franckh.com
www.happiness-house.de
www.michaela-merten.com
www.paulparry.com
www.thedesirecodebook.com

The **Desire Code**

Pierre Franckh

DISCLAIMER:

Every effort has been made to accurately represent the ideas in this book which have been proven to work on many, many occasions by a great number of people. *Successful wishing* and the *Desire Code* are principles which the author has used to help create a prosperous life for himself, his family, coaching clients and also paying attendees of his seminars. However, in life and as we all know, sometimes things don't always turn out as we expected. Therefore, the author cannot accept, under any circumstances, any liability for wishes of any description that are not fulfilled and/or any adverse circumstances that may be perceived as manifesting as a result of implementing ideas contained within this book. Examples in this material are not to be interpreted as a promise or guarantee of any particular circumstances, desired or otherwise. Any claims made by the author of actual *successful wishing* or examples of actual results can be verified upon request. Wishes are as diverse as individuals' personalities. Therefore, the author cannot guarantee your success through your wishing. Nor is the author responsible for any of your actions.

Contents

The **Desire Code**: Key 3 – Thanking

The **Desire Code**: Key 4 – Convince the mind

The **Desire Code**: Key 5 – Have faith instead of doubts

The **Desire Code: Key 6** –
Be open to 'coincidences'

The **Desire Code: Key 7** –
Discover your true great wishes

Foreword

My story

My first wish was fulfilled when I was six years old. I had written a note to my guardian angel and hidden it carefully so that my mother wouldn't find it. The wish came true, nonetheless. I got exactly the bike I wanted – right down to the color and the bell with *Die Maus* (*the Mouse*, a German cartoon character) on it.

By the time I was nine, I no longer believed that wishes come true, I already *knew* it – my own wishes, at any rate. In those three years I had written down many wishes on pieces of paper and had them fulfilled. To me, miracles weren't a matter of faith – they were reality.

All the same, this little boy wanted to put the whole thing to the test. Just to be quite certain, I had to try out something 'impossible', something that technically speaking couldn't work. And so I placed an order with the 'beings up there' for a role in a cinema film. It was to be a real role, with my name appearing in the credits. In my wish note I wrote at the time: "... that everyone would be able to see me well." And indeed, that same year, I co-starred in the film *Lausbubengeschichten* (*Little Rascals Stories*).

My parents thought it was a miracle – I thought of my order, which no one else took seriously.

I took it very seriously indeed, as unfortunately the order had been delivered with greater accuracy than I had anticipated. I had made a small but crucial mistake: in my wish note I had written that everyone was to be able to see me in the film. I hadn't mentioned being *heard*.

During the shooting, the film director changed my character to a Prussian boy who spoke in a Berlin dialect. To my dismay I was dubbed; in the final cut of the film, my lines were spoken by someone else. So I had gotten my first big cinema role, and my wish had been fulfilled to the letter. Everyone could see me, but no one could hear me.

I could hardly imagine more convincing – and, unfortunately, more painful – proof of inaccurate wishing. For this reason, I devote an entire chapter to the correct formulation of a wish.

For a while, I cursed those 'beings up there' – until I realized they were blameless. They simply spoke a different language than I did. They didn't know what was good or bad from my perspective. They had no experience of how things worked here on earth; they just carried out my instructions. From then on, I had no more doubts:

Wishes are fulfilled –
and you get exactly what you ask for.

As a child I knew that. As a child I was still in touch with my wishes, and quite simply expected them to manifest according to my imagination. My little wish-note factory worked back then, at any rate.

But the boy grew and at a certain point started feeling grown-up. And so the little boy, who possessed a greater knowing as a child than later as an adult, became a skeptic and a 'realist'.

On the road to adolescence, he had at some point started believing all those adults more than he believed himself. His talent for 'wishing' fell further and further into oblivion. In his adult world, he wanted to achieve something on his own; he wanted to be proud of himself.

He believed in his own power and regarded the help of others – especially those 'beings up there' – as ridiculous and embarrassing. The little boy had ceased to allow miracles into his life. His life became more difficult, more serious and he often encountered insurmountable obstacles. I started struggling and comparing myself more frequently with others – and concluding that I apparently always had the worst hand.

That the world is unjust had become certain to me: why else do some people succeed at everything and others always fail? Why do some people always have so much 'luck', while others have a patent on things going wrong? Why are some people so incredibly fortunate and others not fortunate in the least?

The answer to these questions – and the turning point in my life – presented itself to me years later when I happened upon a small white book with the title *Wunder* (the German translation of *Miracles*). In this book, Stuart Wilde relates exactly the same experiences that I had had as a child. He calls this singular form of wishing "ordering" – a wonderfully apt expression – and claims that it works for everyone at any time.

I was deeply touched. I began to remember my childhood. Back then, all those miracles that Stuart Wilde spoke of had been possible. They had simply been at my disposal.

But why should all this be available only to a child? Why not to an adult? Was life perhaps less unjust than I had thought?

Could it be that the only difference between winners and losers was that the former never doubted themselves or their wishes? They simply knew that they were entitled to what they were wishing for. It was normal to them that what they had imagined came true. Their thoughts manifested – constantly. But how did they 'think' so differently from others?

> Successful people have no doubts and are always positively focused on their goals.

Ultimately there is only one difference. Some people wish consciously and with focus. Others wish without conscious intention or coordination – and without realizing that they too are creating their own circumstances.

Stuart Wilde's book changed my life completely. Since reading it, I have submitted countless *successful wishes*, like I used to during my childhood. And it works! All you need to do is just start wishing – life can indeed be that simple – while being aware of the dos and don'ts. *Successful wishing* does require you to follow certain rules: the *Desire Code*.

The Desire Code takes some learning

Wishes are fulfilled, every day, every hour, every minute. My wishes, your wishes – all of them. That does mean, though, that our doubts manifest as well, and also our thoughts about our own inadequacy. After all, the latter are wishes too, despite being unintentional. And so they manifest, nonetheless.

For this reason I started observing myself closely. I was, of course, particularly interested in my subconscious wishes and how I could keep them under control.

Our expectations often result in disappointment because we expect to be disappointed.

You see, the Universe cannot distinguish between good and bad. It simply delivers. It doesn't care whether the manifestation of your wish has a positive or a negative impact on your life. The Universe has no notion of just or unjust, good or bad, positive or negative. The Universe simply delivers according to our specifications.

The Universe? What is that supposed to be? Well, from a wishing perspective it is convenient to imagine the Universe as a gigantic online shop. Wishing works on exactly the same principle: our wishes are processed and delivered.

I'll deal with the actual quantum physics of wishing later on – that is, the interaction between sending out a wish and having it delivered, and how that relates to the manifestation of energy in the material world. For now, the concept of a Universal online shop is quite helpful in learning the correct way of wishing. Above all, it helps us to approach wishing in a playful way. The advantage of this is that playfulness and ease speed up the fulfillment of the wish.

Regarding playfulness and ease, it's important to know that the Universal online shop always has infinite stocks of everything. Everything is therefore always available to us, and *when we receive something, it doesn't mean that someone else has to do without.* (This doesn't apply, of course, if I wish for my best friend's partner).

In the course of the past thirty years, I have learned a great deal about how *The Desire Code* works. From my own experiences and mistakes – and those of many others – I have distilled seven keys that help us to lead the life we want.

When we wish the *right* way, we manifest anything we want – nothing is impossible or out of our reach. The fascinating thing is that if you set about it the right way, wishing knows no bounds. Whether you want money, a house, a car, a partner, a job or love, everything is possible.

There are no limits.
Limitations exist only in the mind.

It is in the mind that we create our daily world. And because we adults don't know that – or don't *want* to know it – we are generally pretty dissatisfied with the world we have created.

But how do you overcome these limitations? What is the right way to wish? How do you express your wishes clearly and unambiguously, without constantly blocking their delivery or unintentionally wishing for something that you in fact don't want at all? How do you avoid missing the delivery of your wish? And how do you keep dreadful things from happening in your life?

All these questions are repeatedly put to me during my seminars. In the end, though, they all boil down to the same question: how do I allow all the miracles into my life?

Wishes manifest.
What do I want to manifest in my life?

The more often I spoke about *The Desire Code* during my evening seminars, the more interested I became in learning more about this phenomenon. In my audiences there were people who had already heard of the most diverse forms of wishing and actually practiced them for some time. Many of these wishers had at some point given up, however, because it wasn't working for them.

I was astonished. What had become completely normal for me and my life wasn't in the least self-evident to others. And the more I explained, the more questions arose – in my own mind, too. So I started asking my audiences about *their* wishing methods, too. From their answers it became increasingly clear to me why so many people weren't getting their desired outcomes and where they were making mistakes.

This led to people requesting me ever more frequently to finally write a kind of 'user's manual' on *The Desire Code*. So, many thanks to all of you who kept urging me on. Without you, this book would not have been written.

I still recall the lady who smiled at me so sweetly and said, "I know you're going to write that book". "Why?" I replied, taken aback. "Because, I wish it."

The **Desire Code**:

Key 1 – Just start!

The best way to master the art of *successful wishing* is to simply start – with easy 'finger exercises'. After all, we are eager to see our first results as soon as possible.

And what is the fastest way of achieving our first successes? By starting with small wishes.

Why 'small' ones?

Because then we find it easier to approach the whole wishing business in a playful and unbiased manner. Things of less significance are also less fraught with anxiety and doubt. You can see them with your mind's eye and subsequently forget them; that is, let them go and thus send them on their energetic journey. With less important things we are more inclined to trust that the wish will be fulfilled, because the desired outcome matters less to us. And, trust is one of the most important ingredients of *successful wishing*. Trust creates faith.

Faith in the outcome creates the outcome

So the important thing is solely faith in the outcome. Faith is the primary source that continually feeds the wish with energy. It is always faith that moves mountains.

The issue of the mind

The mind, on the other hand, demands logical explanations and will therefore try to convince us that this wishing business cannot work. It doesn't – as yet – know any better. But every new positive experience and each successful outcome will contribute to convincing it that we *do* have the ability to realize our visions. After all, the mind has a tremendous capacity for learning. However, it can know only what it has experienced and what it understands. It is not able or willing to perceive anything else.

For this reason, miracles are not the mind's business. It even tries to prevent, outright, all possible miracles. What doesn't fit into its picture of the world cannot be. As I explain later – with reference to scientific insights for the mind's benefit – this is why our wishes not only *can* be fulfilled, but indeed always *are* fulfilled, without exception. We can point this out to our mind when it is about to start doubting again.

Let's get one thing clear: the same principle applies to great(er) miracles. To the Universe it doesn't matter how big or small our wish is.

It is always merely our imagination
that allows or prevents something.

But given the previous conditioning of our imagination, we do not really believe that our wishes will come true. Consequently our subconscious strongly counteracts the fulfillment of seemingly *large* wishes.

On the contrary, *small* 'miracles' could occur by sheer chance; as the saying goes, "even a blind squirrel finds a nut once in a while". But from this first small 'miracle' we may derive the courage to proceed to the next small miracle – which may not be a miracle at all anymore, but perhaps the successful delivery of our wish. The fourth and fifth miracles provide further confirmation. Our mind realizes that something apparently exists that it cannot explain.

It adapts to the idea and builds a new concept of reality. And suddenly it starts to accept the new world, for *successful wishing* is something the mind can grasp; it sends out and it receives. After a while, it starts viewing itself as a creator, too.

And suddenly we find ourselves believing a key law of physics:

Energy follows attention.

"If this is true," the mind says to itself, "then it follows that one should be able to tackle the larger wishes as well." Certainly. At first, though, it's important to truly convince our mind. And the easiest way to do that is by manifesting small wishes. The only thing we have to bear in mind is to persevere – unwaveringly.

We will therefore start with a short test phase. What we need is a successful outcome in order to show our mind: "Look, it works." We need something tangible that will allow us to release our ingrained belief that it quite simply doesn't work.

Practice makes perfect

We are beginners at the art of conscious *successful wishing*. So let's think of ourselves as apprentices. A goldsmith's apprentice, for example, isn't given the task of making a valuable, brilliant diamond necklace as his first assignment. He knows that this is the goal to which he ultimately seeks to aspire. At the end of his apprenticeship, he is skilled enough to work with valuable materials which require expert handling.

Our goal, likewise, is that wishing comes effortlessly to us – regardless of the magnitude of our wish – and consistently produces the desired outcome. It's therefore a good idea to start by practicing on small wishes and using these to gain experience. Gaining experience includes making mistakes and learning from them – as

I did with my wish for a role in a cinema film. So let's practice with small things that produce fast results.

Reserving a parking space

How about the famous parking space, for example – the one that's always snapped up by someone else right under our nose? The advantages of this are twofold.

First advantage

Parking spaces provide the easiest practice because in their playful character they do not form a serious threat to our existing beliefs. If we were to use *successful wishing* to procure a parking space, this would not immediately shake our thinking system. The reason why this is important is that otherwise our mind would smell danger, in its role as 'chief thinker', and might try to sabotage our wish.

But a parking space is more of a fun thing, more of a game. Even if it were to really work, to our mind that wouldn't prove anything.

Second advantage

In addition, a parking space isn't really so important that we might think, "We don't deserve it". With large wishes it's very different. When we wish for something that is really important to us, we are quick to start doubting and believing that our wish won't manifest because we are secretly convinced that we are not entitled to such wonderful things. "I'm not beautiful, clever, rich or intelligent enough for that."

Obtaining a parking space, however, has a playful character. It's not something to take really seriously. And that is precisely what we want to take advantage of.

So how do we do that?

My order for a parking space

When I leave my house, I send out a short request, which – for simplicity's sake – I address to the Parking Space Angel. I could, of course, equally well say, "Dear Cosmos", "Dear Universe" or "Dear Wishing Energy".

Ultimately it doesn't matter what you choose to call it. What matters is that it works. For myself, I prefer the angels. I find them more personal and intimate. Whatever entity you address your wishes to, remember these important points: don't make fun of it, don't doubt and don't dismiss *successful wishing* as nonsense. After all, we want a parking space and this is a trial run. During a trial run it's okay to do unusual things.

"Okay, dear Parking Space Angel. I have a parking space in ... Street. It's already destined for me. I will get it at the exact moment that I arrive there."

Avoid stating your wish too shortly before its intended manifestation, as even the Universe needs some time to prepare things. The best moment to express your wish is on leaving your house.

And…it works!!

Today we shall believe that. Today we shall test the power of our thoughts and see how simple life can be. On our way to … Street we should not give more thought to our wish than necessary – preferably none at all. When you lack practice at *successful wishing*, doubts are more likely to arise than the certainty that everything is working in your best interests.

In any case the fact is that when we arrive at our destination, the miracle will manifest. Either there will be a free parking space already available precisely where we need it, or someone will be driving away just as we arrive.

Since Michaela, my wife, and I have been *successfully wishing*, we have had no trouble at all finding a parking space. Not for decades! Nowadays we submit our request almost without thinking about it, because we know that our communication line is open and our wish will arrive.

Sometimes it even happens that I don't see my allocated parking space at first, and ask 'up there' for further directions or a sign. That works, too. Someone either sounds their horn or behaves so conspicuously that my attention is drawn there.

But things don't always go perfectly. We sometimes forget to wish, and then we end up laughing heartily on finding parked cars everywhere. In such situations I always ask Michaela, "Did you perhaps order our parking space a bit late?" And she always replies, "I thought that *you* had ordered one ages ago."

It's at times like these that the difference between *successful wishing* and struggling through life on one's own suddenly becomes so clear again.

> Joining forces with the Universe
> is considerably easier than
> struggling along on your own.

So, let's make use of this power that is always available to all of us – even if we merely wish to secure a parking space.

Michaela and I have been facilitating our everyday lives for so long with these little wishes that we have come to regard them as a matter of course. We could fill a whole book with all these little 'miracles' we have manifested so far.

In search of plants

It so happened that a few years ago we wanted some plants for our cozy home. Large ones, of course. Preferably ceiling-high. We went to DIY stores, garden centers and nurseries. We soon realized, however, that what we had in mind was beyond our financial means. Great flourishing palm trees and other plants cost a fortune, to say nothing of beautiful plant pots.

So there were only three things left to do: wish, give thanks and trust.

Just a week later, the phone rang. A friend of ours asked us whether we would like to accompany him. A medium-sized business had gone bankrupt and was selling its furniture. Now we weren't particularly interested in office furniture, but our friend could use some extra pairs of hands.

When we entered the office building, everything became clear in an instant. Great big enormous plants smiled at us from magnificent huge plant pots. And because no one else wanted them, the curator let us have them for next to nothing. We rented a truck and drove them home the same day. Those plants were really so big that we had to make room for them at home.

Choose some little wishes of your own to practice on. Manifest them successfully; convince yourself and your mind; gain confidence. Then you will be able to deal confidently with larger wishes.

You must just do it – even though you may feel ridiculous at first. By the way, it's only your mind that thinks you're being ridiculous. But your mind quite simply isn't responsible for 'miracles'.

The **Desire Code**:

Key 2 – Get the wording right

The 'I am' principle

The biggest mistake people make over and over again when wishing is that their *choice of words* sends out an entirely different message than they intend. In spite of all their good intentions, this doesn't bring them any closer to their goals – on the contrary. Usually people word their wishes in such a way that they set in stone more indelibly than ever the unfortunate state in which they find themselves.

If you wish for a lot of money, for example, then it's totally wrong to state your wish as "*I want to* have a lot of money". What you will get in that case is the state of "I want to be rich". That state we already know. It is the state of "wanting something" and "not having". This wording, therefore, merely reinforces our state of lack.

Create the state of "being or having something",
instead of the state of "wanting something".

So, the right wording is "I am ready for wealth in my life", or "I am rich and happy", or "the money that is meant for me is already there and it is now finding the right way to appear in my life".

Our wish statement is: "*I am* rich" not "*I want to be* rich".

If we're in search of a relationship, we must not wish: "I want to have the right partner in my life" or "I would like to meet the right partner". That way, everything will stay as it is.

As the Universe understands it, we want something, and so it sends us a state of wanting. The Universe makes no distinction between the present and the future. It delivers that which we are now thinking and feeling. That has the following implication for the wording of our wish statements:

> We always wish in the present –
> and not the future – tense.

"I want to be happy" unfortunately brings us exactly that: the wanting. We will continue to *want* happiness. The Universe understands that it is our wish to want something. "I am happy" is the wording that brings us the state we are actually wishing for.

"I am open and ready to allow love into my life" opens doors. The searching is over. "I know that the right partner is already out there and is now coming into my life" draws the right person into my life.

Pretending (acting 'as if')

When wishing for a new cupboard for our living room, the best way to start is by clearing out the old cupboard and giving it away or having someone come and take it away. We are assuming that our wish for a new cupboard is already being processed. On a vibrational level, we have already 'bought' the cupboard. So, it already exists somewhere and it's just a matter of time before the new cupboard appears in our living room.

Pretending, or acting as if, compels the Universe to deliver. The more clearly our wish already exists in our imagination, the faster the Universe must resolve the curious discrepancy between our thoughts and reality.

That which we want, we already have.

In this way, we increase the pressure of our wish hugely. The energy we send out is so strong that the order is placed right on top of our 'account manager''s stack – regardless of whether we want a cupboard, money or a new partner.

The more we act as if we were already rich or in the desired relationship, the faster our wish will manifest, because we are sending out an incredibly powerful energy. We are actually drawing the objects of our desire into our lives.

That doesn't mean that if we want to be rich, we must spend large amounts of money up front and overdraw our bank accounts. It's more about *feeling* rich, and wealth already being part of our lives.

We can affirm these wishes by pretending that they have already manifested. Why is this acting-as-if so important? Because in doing so we are continually focusing, in a positive way, on what we are in the process of manifesting, and expectantly tuning in to it. In other words, we are getting ourselves on the right vibrational frequency.

Furthermore, our doubts subside, we reinforce our faith and feel on a purely emotional level how great this manifestation will be for us. At the same time we are giving the mind little room to look for counterarguments, eliminating every attempt it makes to convince us how impossible our intentions are. We counterbalance with the experience of joy and vitality that is manifesting in our lives as our wish unfolds: "That's how it feels when our wish is fulfilled." Emotions are always stronger and more intense than rational arguments of the mind.

Anticipating the feeling of fulfillment fortifies us in our wish and helps to keep us from faltering.

Above all, though, we shift from a consciousness of lack to one of abundance. That which we want is already ours, because we are entitled to it. We are no longer creating emotional or financial lack; instead, we perceive every event or encounter as something that brings us closer to our wish.

"Not" and "no" – the 'fear' thing

Beware of wishes where you feel a good deal of fear lurking in the background. Fear is a huge magnet.

Fear attracts precisely the things that
we are seeking to avoid.

Fearful thoughts have a very strong emotional charge, which gives them an exceptionally powerful energy. Besides, we occupy ourselves particularly extensively with the things we fear. We are continually imagining the worst possible scenarios in vivid detail and replaying them over and over again in our mind's eye.

Despite our fear, we give these scenarios more time and attention than we spend on the pleasant aspects of our lives. Even when we are well and things are working out fine, we often fail to recognize the miracles in our lives, immersing ourselves instead in dull anxiety.

Energy, however, always follows attention. This means that we always attract the things we focus our attention on.

Yet that is precisely what we do not want to do. Strictly speaking, we want the exact opposite: to avoid all things terrible.

Everything that we try to avoid,
we draw into our lives.

When we wish in a fear-laden way, we are in fact trying to avoid or escape something. No matter how positively we seek to express our wish, the real underlying thought is usually: "I don't want to be .../to have .../... to happen."

The Universe, however, doesn't know the words 'not' and 'no'. It can't make anything of wishes stated in the negative, nor of attempts to avoid (in other words: *not do*) something.

A wish containing a denial will virtually always manifest the exact opposite of what we are actually wishing for. The Universe quite simply deletes the words 'not' and 'no' from our order forms and literally delivers what remains, as if that is the way we want it.

In terms of wishing energy, "I don't want to be ill" means "I (do) want to be ill". Why is this so?

Well, we cannot cause something to *not* come into being. We can only *create something*. The mere thought of 'not creating' brings into existence precisely what we don't want.

The Universe doesn't know the word 'not' and therefore deletes it. Wishing to not *be* or *do* or *have* something reinforces our fear of that thing – and, consequently, delivers it to us.

The wish suggests that the fear of falling ill is substantially greater than our desire to be healthy.

So, wanting to avoid something doesn't work. But we can manifest the opposite of that something. We must therefore focus on its positive equivalent. The command that is understood 'up there' is "I am healthy". This wording is simple and clear. With this wish, our focus is on our health and not on illness.

But let's be honest. How many such negative wishes do we think and say every day? "I don't want to lose my job." "I don't want to die." "I don't want to have an accident." "I don't want my partner to leave me." "I don't want to be poor."

We are thus effectively occupying ourselves solely with the negative aspects and sending out the corresponding energy – which is interpreted accordingly 'up there', as we now know.

Correctly stated wishes are: "I have a job"; "I am happy in my relationship"; "I have everything I need".

You will now probably understand why certain wishes were seemingly delivered incorrectly. In reality the delivery was not incorrect – it was actually very prompt and exactly as ordered. It's just that the order form had been filled in incorrectly.

Write the wish down

This amplifies the wish. It physically leaves our body for the first time. Just by doing so it gains power. Suddenly we're being serious. We have left the realm of speculation and dreams, in which we don't yet quite believe in the wish.

When we write our wish down, we manifest it.

From now on it is in the material world. It is our firm intention. Imperturbable, clear and unambiguous.

In particular, those who are new to wishing should commit their wishes to paper. Later on, when you have established a routine and reinforced your faith with a sufficient number of successful manifestations, you can occasionally afford to skip the writing down step. In those cases you can simply make an impromptu wish, or with a brief glance to the heavens, or in whatever way occurs to you.

Casual wishing does have a drawback, however; sooner or later we will inevitably lose track of all the things we have been wishing for.

Besides, not only are we wishing for something or other in passing all the time, but we are also continually augmenting, modifying and (partially) canceling our wishes. Often we didn't really mean what we were wishing – we were just momentarily inspired by it and the next moment we want something entirely different.

To the Universe, that doesn't matter. What we wish for is delivered, even though we may no longer have any use for it, or could indeed happily do without it. And so we suddenly find ourselves with a glut of sent-out wishes and we have no overview of our own lives. Countless different and contradictory things happen around us, and in the general chaos we no longer recognize that we are the creators of everything.

On top of that, there are all our subconscious wishes, which we certainly don't want to manifest in the least.

And so we are back where we didn't want to be anymore: things manifesting and we have no idea who commissioned them.

We would therefore do well to manifest our first wishes quite consciously – and to give them a clear direction and weight by writing them down. And to begin with, at any rate, I would advise you to create a little ritual for this.

My wish is worth my time and attention.

So, let this moment become a special moment. Take your time and choose a quiet place. In this moment you are creating your life. You may want to put on pleasing music, light a few candles or just remain in total silence. It's important that you relax.

When we are relaxed, life seems much more pleasant and our wish takes shape in a considerably more positive way. And positive thoughts are a catalyst for our wishing energy. We shall discuss in detail later on why this is so.

When you have formulated your wish quite clearly for yourself, write it down – in the deep inner knowing that it will now be fulfilled.

Fold the piece of paper together and put it in a special place. This place should be a beautiful one, for it shows us how important and 'sacred' our wish is to us. By all means choose a secret place that no other eyes will see. What is important is that we are aware of the power of the wish we have sent out, and one of the ways of affirming this is by choosing a special place for our little note.

Writing the wish down on a sheet of paper, on a card or in our diary is marvelous proof for our mind (we usually don't recall with complete accuracy what we have written down). While we do remember the general essence of our wish, the words have a way of becoming skewed in our mind over time. No wonder, given that every day we are deluged with countless new influences. We ourselves change, our thoughts change and therefore so does our memory, which mostly deludes us with an inseparable mixture of truth, thoughts and hopes.

If, upon delivery of the wish, you can refer back to the original order, you often experience a wondrous surprise. You will be utterly amazed at how strictly according to your written specifications the wish has indeed manifested.

Without a written record of your wish, on the other hand, you are certain to run into a large number of unsolvable riddles. That's what happened to me, at least. Although my wish had been fulfilled to the letter, I couldn't make anything of it at first because I hadn't written the wish down and in my joy at its fulfillment I had, of course, forgotten the precise wording.

The gift box has arrived, but can't be opened

Some ten years ago, after our film *And That's Only the Beginning*, we were almost broke. We had invested all our money in our own production company and, although the film did amazingly well, it didn't generate enough box office revenues. Furthermore, Michaela and I had worked on a provisional basis, which is to say that we had waived a large part of our salaries for the benefit of the film.

After exhausting all our financial possibilities, we were finally forced to close down our company, and our financial prospects weren't clear. We could have put it somewhat more drastically: we had lost everything and were facing a rigorous new start. The situation was more than tense.

My income as an author was not yet sufficient to live on and, when the last of our savings dwindled more rapidly than we had anticipated, I was gradually overcome with panic and I confided all my worries to Michaela. I envisioned the most dreadful scenarios, and in my fearful hopelessness I described them (in my opinion, at least) very convincingly to her.

I made it unmistakably clear to her that we would either have to take up acting again immediately, or else give notice that we would be moving out of our expensive house. The best thing would be to relocate to a small flat as soon as possible. Only then would we stand a chance of keeping our expenses within affordable limits until I could perhaps start making money from my writing.

Michaela just smiled. And when Michaela smiles, no one can refuse her anything in the world. At least, *I* can't. When Michaela smiles, her soul smiles and you know that everything will be fine.

At the same time, however, it was clear to me that none of my proposed solutions would be adopted.

The only conceivable solution, according to Michaela, was that we submit a success-guaranteed wish to the Universe. Michaela has been doing this since the age of eleven, and the wonderful thing about her is that virtually nothing daunts her. After all, she has a staunch ally in her life – not counting me, of course – in the form of the Universe.

When Michaela and I met for the first time, then, it was an encounter between two active 'wishers'. And whenever one of us happens to be down, the other peps up the other, whereupon we remind each other that we actually don't have to do anything except utilize our wishing power.

On that particular evening, it was Michaela who smilingly proposed the only truly sensible solution. We just had to practice the *Desire Code* and *wish successfully.*

When all else fails, wishing always works.

Of course. How could I have forgotten that? The conviction that Michaela radiated was in itself sufficient to restore my innate faith.

If writing were really my 'thing', and I were to continue doing it in the future, then the Universe would have to furnish the means of financial security. It was therefore obvious that my order would be registered and promptly delivered. Back then, I used to think that I needed this kind of justification for my wishes.

How much money did I need? How long would we have to live on it? What would be a nice sum? How much money had we lost on our production company? How much money had I foregone by waiving a large part of my director's and author's salary?

This money was to allow us to live free of financial worries for at least a year, and it was to approximately equal the sum that I had waived for our film.

By my calculations, that amounted to about 80,000 Deutschmarks (approximately US$45,000). But a truly beautiful sum would be DM 77,777. So, our wish was finally clear.

I gave thanks in advance for the fulfillment of the wish; I was certain that the money would arrive and didn't want to give it any further thought, let alone be tempted to start having doubts. My wish was to retain its power and energy.

Several weeks later we were both invited to the UNES-CO Gala in Düsseldorf to sell lottery tickets for a fundraising campaign.

As always, we bought a few for ourselves. We waited... and waited, but nothing. Not even a book or a hairdryer or even a ridiculous CD. All the prizes had been drawn and awarded to the delighted winners – except the first prize: a brand new Jaguar.

Suddenly, in the split second that the giant wheel of fortune started spinning for the last time, I knew that my wish was on the verge of manifesting. This was the big moment. In this instant, I felt aware of the Universe and all its gifts. I knew that in this moment my wish would be fulfilled. I felt connected and aligned with the entire Universe. I stammered: "Oh my God, now it's going to happen," and Michaela stared at me with a baffled expression.

And yet – even though I had 'anticipated' it – I was just as stunned as Michaela when Kai Pflaume, the host for the evening, called the number of my ticket. Kai was so astonished to see me on the stage that he checked my ticket several times. But there was no doubt about it. The main prize of the evening, a Jaguar worth DM 111,000, was mine.

And then the question arose as to the price we could obtain for the car, as it was clear to both me and Michaela that we didn't want to keep it. The proceeds from its sale were, after all, intended to finance my writing career. A renowned car dealer would sell the car on our behalf, and set the price at DM 104,000.

A week went by, then another week, and yet another. The car was not sold. Plenty of customers came to the showroom, but they all ignored our car and purchased the same model, but at the full price.

After three weeks, we had the price lowered to DM 99,000. The car dealer people weren't particularly enthusiastic about that. They feared that they would be trampling on their own prices. However, in the end they gave in to my pressure. A week went by, then another, and the car was not sold.

After a lengthy struggle the price was lowered once more, this time to DM 88,000. In vain. The car remained unsalable. No one understood why. The car was a bargain and there was no shortage of customers at the car dealer's, but no one wanted our car, which by then stood directly at the entrance to the showroom. Not even for DM 85,000.

Michaela and I were totally confused. The money we were wishing for was practically under our very noses but there didn't seem to be any way for it to come to us.

And yet the solution surely had to be simple. After all, we had so far always been successful in our wishing. That I had won the car was proof enough. Nevertheless, we didn't understand what was going wrong here. So we just sat down quietly and inquired inside.

And then it hit me like a bolt of lightning. We didn't *understand* it. But the mind can rarely be of help where successful deliveries from the Universe are concerned. Mostly it is our intuition that shows us the right path. The answer was as logical as it was obvious. I had asked for a sum that would offset the missed revenues from our film and provide us with a year's subsistence.

The sum I had requested was about DM 80,000. Or was it? And then – of course – I remembered. I had liked the repetition of the divine number 7. That is to say, the precise sum I had wished for was DM 77,777 which, at the time of writing, is approximately $43,000.

I frantically phoned the car dealer, but the people there weren't thrilled at my latest pricing suggestion. They refused to give the car away so cheaply. Only after a prolonged dispute did they reluctantly do as I asked.

A week went by, then another week, and the car was not sold. I was at a loss to understand what was going on. Now we had surely got everything right – so why was my order not being delivered?

I phoned again. Had the car dealer really changed the price on the label to DM 77,777? After a considerable discussion they admitted that I would indeed receive DM 77,777 from them, but that they did want to make a bit of profit for themselves and had therefore adjusted the price to DM 82,000. Only when I vehemently insisted that they state the agreed-upon sum on the price label did they back down – perhaps for no other reason than to finally be rid of me.

Less than two hours later I received a phone call. At the price of DM 77,777, the car had been sold immediately.

In the midst of my joy, I did start to feel a bit annoyed. Why had I (idiot that I was) not wished for DM 88,888 or DM 99,999 – or for enough to live off for two years instead of one? Then I would have gotten considerably more for the Jaguar.

But would I have actually received more than the DM 77,777? This sum sufficed to make ends meet comfortably for the both of us. Probably it was precisely the sum I was entitled to. Or was it simply a case of the Universe delivering exactly to specifications?

Or was it just a string of coincidences?

The amazing thing about this story is this: less than a year earlier, my wonderful Michaela had also won a car! A small red Toyota, which we still drive today.

How did that come about? Well, Michaela would say that a few weeks previously she had wished for this car from the Universe. I'll tell you more about that miraculous lottery win later on.

But let's return to the Jaguar. Had I written down my wish, I would have spared myself a fair amount of brain racking and several weeks' wait into the bargain. When the wish manifested, I simply wasn't entirely clear anymore about what I had actually, exactly wished for.

Another thing that happens quite often is that certain parts of the delivery are not or no longer to our liking. Perhaps we hadn't ever intended them that way. In those cases, we are often totally convinced that the order was delivered incorrectly. Our written record, however, documents the original wording of the wish and shows us how accurately the Universe operates and how inaccurately we had stated our wish.

It is precisely by writing the wish down that you learn, within a short period of time, to deal with the difference between what you wished for and what was actually delivered. These comparisons will soon enable you to state your wishes so specifically that life will unfold miraculously before you. When you choose the right wording, *successful wishing* is quite simple.

In any case, writing our desire down is evidence that our little wish factory works and isn't just a figment of our imagination. In a short space of time we will have accumulated a large number of these little notes, and our initial doubt will have transformed first into trusting amazement and ultimately into convinced knowing.

Nothing is as successful as success itself,
for it begets more success.

When I took up wishing again, I collected many such little notes. Having attended a grammar school specializing in natural sciences, I needed a lot of this kind of evidence. Such schools are well known for churning out skeptical realists. I therefore required a certain amount of time to re-educate my mind and convince it of the effectiveness of wishing. But in the end the notes were powerful enough to win over even my mind. It understood that wishing works, and henceforth operated in the desired direction.

I like working with notes, by the way. Both longitudinal walls of my study are covered with bulletin boards, rendering the 'creative chaos' manageable. But having bits of paper everywhere is not everyone's cup of tea, and many people tell me that they prefer to write down their wishes in a special wishing journal, or in a different color in their regular diary.

This approach does indeed have several advantages. Firstly, you can understand later on how the wish evolved, from the initial vague, "I want a lot of ..." to the definitive version. This allows you to skip many intermediate steps the next time round.

A further advantage is that you can always refer back to the wishes and the way they were fulfilled – even years later. Not only can you draw valuable lessons for your future wishing from past experiences, but you also have irrefutable evidence, in black and white, for your mind, should it start having doubts again and ascribing everything to 'chance'.

In addition, the written records will, time after time, provide an incentive to make yet another successful wish. This possibility doesn't always spring to mind, especially when you are up to your neck in difficulties.

And last but not least: it's simply fun to write down all your success stories!

State your wish clearly, concisely and precisely

The more accurately you specify your wish, the more accurately it is delivered. The more vaguely you set about wishing, the greater the possibility that you will get something other than what you actually had in mind.

For example, if you want a cupboard for your living room, then describe its appearance and where you want to put it, the color, the kind of wood, the dimensions and also what objects you will want to keep in it. If you aren't sufficiently precise, there will be too much leeway between your thoughts and the manifestation, and you may well get a cupboard that doesn't suit your purposes at all.

No matter how many items our order consists of and how detailed our specifications are, each item will be duly delivered.

Nevertheless, on the delivery of our wish we sometimes realize – to our great annoyance – that we had overlooked certain other relevant details. It is therefore not all that important to draw up a thousand-item catalog, for there will always be a hundred thousand more items that we had failed to consider, and that have now been added to the delivery in a manner not particularly to our liking.

Try to express it in two or three sentences.

That sounds like a contradiction – but it isn't. The more precisely and briefly you must state the wish, the more you are compelled to come to the actual essence of it. If you are able to express it in two sentences, you are far clearer on what you are really wishing for.

A scriptwriter seeking to present his idea to a producer will always be requested to express it in one sentence. If you can't get your story across in a few words, there is no way you'll manage it using many words.

That is why authors often spend a very long time expressing the basic idea of the story as concisely as possible. Copywriters, sometimes restricted to two or three words, face the same challenge. Yet these few words must convey the essence precisely.

The more concisely you express it, then, the more precise the wish will be. The more words you need, the more ambiguous and vague your order – and hence the delivery – will be. A short, to-the-point wish statement is substantially more powerful than a two-page essay.

My own experience has shown time and time again just how powerful a few little words can be.

An unintended –
and yet successful – wish

At the age of 22 I was already very famous from my TV appearances – but not at the theater. TV and theater were incompatible at that time. In the theater world, TV actors were scorned and regarded as second-rate.

It was therefore extremely unlikely that a TV star like me would ever get a good role in a renowned theater.

One day, however, I saw a performance of *Hamlet* at the Residenztheater (Residence Theater in Munich), featuring Michael Degen. It made a lasting impression on me and I absolutely wanted to perform at this theater myself. An impossible venture. I didn't even manage to get an appointment with the artistic director, Kurt Meisel, or the playwright.

This annoyed me so much that I vented all my frustration on a large sheet of paper. Enraged, I wrote: "I am performing at this theater! This year! And in a role of my own choosing!"

And to allow everyone to see my indignation, I pinned this sheet of paper to my bulletin board. Short, precise and unerring. And I was convinced that it would manifest.

Three months later, the Residenztheater phoned me. They wanted me to come and see them. What had happened? Michael Degen was staging *Faust 1* and *Faust 2* (you may know it as *Doctor Faustus*), and instead of drawing on the theater's own actors, he wanted to cast new, fresh people – actors like me. So I auditioned with him – initially for the role of the theater director in *Faust 1*.

Michael Degen sent me home and three days later auditioned me for the part of the Scholar. And then he indeed asked me which role I preferred and which one I would like to play, the Horse-courser, the Clown or the Scholar.

I asked for some time to think it over, and consulted my father. He advised me to play the Scholar, a classical role that would develop into a major character in *Faust 2*.

And so it came to pass that I performed at the Residenztheater in Munich that same year, in a role that I had chosen myself.

That same week I sat with artistic director Kurt Meisel, who offered me a three-year contract. However, I didn't want to commit myself to one theater for that long. I had seen all those colleagues who were informed about the roles assigned to them through postings on the noticeboard. I was just too freethinking to subject myself to that.

Without being aware of it, back then I had already wished very precisely and specifically, and manifested my wish by means of a note on my bulletin board. I didn't have the slightest doubt that this outcome was inevitable.

The **Desire Code**:

Key 3 – Thanking

After committing our wish to paper, we complete our order by giving thanks. This is very important. Thanking holds so many positive aspects for our *successful wishing* that I can only touch on them briefly here.

Multiplying the good things

Giving thanks invites us to start reflecting on the things in our lives that are going well. We turn our attention to the wonderful happenings that occur in our everyday lives. We look at them with respect and recognition. This in itself makes us acknowledge that an incredible number of things in our lives are already perfectly fine. We become aware of how much we have so far taken for granted, and how much attention we lavish on the few things that, perhaps, are not quite in order yet.

If we were to spontaneously draw up a small list of all the things that are working out well in our lives, we would be astonished at how long this list turns out to be.

It's often the case that eight out of ten things are running just beautifully but we keep on staring at the few negative aspects. This will of course result in the negative things becoming more important and wonderful things will diminish more and more. If we always focus only on displeasing things, then at some point our whole lives will cease to please us.

> Continually focusing on what you lack
> distorts your perception of your wealth.

Perhaps we are basically just too focused on the negative. Or we spend too much time comparing ourselves to others – it's the comparison that makes us unhappy.

Strangely enough, we always see only the positive aspects in others. We succumb to feelings of inferiority because we *believe* – wrongly – that we can't have all that stuff, too (materialistic things as well as success, happiness, wealth, health and so on).

The following exercise is quite helpful when we want to take a look at ourselves from the outside.

> *Choose a quiet moment, sit down comfortably and relax. Focus your attention on yourself. Contemplate yourself with a smile and recall all the beautiful moments in your life. How much have you already achieved? What have you accomplished so far? How many people have you helped? Who are all the people who owe their happiness to you?*

Contemplate yourself once again in these wonderful moments of your life. View them without melancholy. All these things you were capable of in the past. That is your power, your talent and your ability. You will be capable of that in the future, too. You can achieve all that again and again.

And now contemplate yourself in your surroundings. Contemplate your family, your friends, your relatives. You are important to them – because you are of significance in their lives. Your love for them is your wealth. You are a mainstay and example to them. Through the power of your words, through each of your actions, you change their lives as well. Thanks to you they accomplish a great deal that they might not have accomplished without you – your encouragement, your care and your love. Often enough it was quite simply just your mere presence. Feel gratitude for the opportunities that life has so far offered you to show your greatness.

And now focus on the moments in which your friends and acquaintances and your family have helped you in the past. How many people think well of you? How many love you, even though they may not always be able to show it? How much strength and joy do they give you? How often do they fight with you for the truth, because you are important to them?

And then contemplate yourself in your immediate surroundings.

How wonderful that you have made it to here – in spite of sometimes very adverse circumstances! Look around you in your mind's eye. All this you have created from scratch. You are the creator of your own world. Contemplate yourself with kindness and warmth. Life, too, is generous with its gifts to you. Feel how wonderful all this is. Feel your gratitude.

And now open your eyes and start writing all these wonderful things down in a little list. You will be amazed at how much is already turning out marvelously in your life.

With this exercise we start up a different type of energy circulation. Instead of always brooding over our problems, we acknowledge the good things that are already present in our lives. The more often we do this exercise, the more clearly we recognize the things in our lives that are working for us. We realize that our lives are already flowing freely in many respects.

> Thanking causes all that is wonderful
> in our lives to multiply.

What we focus our attention on, we feed with energy. By thanking, we cause all the good things that are already present in our lives to multiply, because we feed them even more energy. Life becomes more and more wonderful, because we are focusing our awareness on what is beautiful in our lives. Gratitude fills our hearts. Gratitude transforms us into pure sources of energy. The clearer and purer the energy is, the faster and more precisely all our wishes can take effect.

Drawing the wish into the present

However, the fundamental idea behind giving thanks is not just to connect with the Universe and the flow of life, but also to draw the desired outcome into the present.

The moment we give thanks, the wish is heard and immediately manifests – because thanking moves the wish into the present. It's similar to saying "Amen" at the end of a prayer. "Amen" translates as "Truly, certainly!". Thus it now is.

The energies of prayer and wish are very similar. In both cases we call on a higher order and request a solution, sealing or concluding our request with "Amen" or our thanks.

Reinforcing the faith

Giving thanks also eliminates all doubts and worries. We believe that the wish will be carried out. We are sure of that. As in everyday life, we give thanks only for things that have already been confirmed. "Thank you for doing that for me."

In other words, thanking is something we do only in situations where we are absolutely certain that the other party will bring about the desired outcome.

By thanking we confirm our order. The wish is sealed. It's like the signature on a document. Now there is no longer any room for doubt. This works even in the most hopeless of situations, as Michaela and I have repeatedly been allowed to experience.

As I mentioned earlier, Michaela and I once won two cars within the space of a year. I've already recounted the amazing story of how I won the Jaguar. Less than twelve months earlier, a very similar 'miracle' had occurred.

The wished-for car

Michaela had an accident with our old second car, and we sold the badly dented vehicle. At this time, however, I had to drive daily from Bonn to Cologne for the preparations of our film, *And That's Only the Beginning*. We therefore urgently needed a second car for Michaela. But how were we to obtain one? Quite simply: by wishing.

Instead of being annoyed about the accident, we welcomed the change in our lives and were ready to allow a new car to find us. How? That wasn't supposed to be our problem anymore.

Several weeks later, our wish long since forgotten, we were invited to a gala in Cologne, where we obligingly bought lottery tickets for charity. We waited seemingly forever for the draw, but in the end we were so tired that we gave the tickets to a couple we knew and went home.

The next morning our friend phoned us while we were still in bed, saying he would drop by shortly. One of our lottery tickets had won a prize – admittedly only a small one, but he wanted to deliver it to us personally.

Our friend arrived during a casting session in our kitchen. We had set up a small camera there, and Clelia Sarto was auditioning for a part in our new film. The prize that our friend held up for all to see was indeed small. It was a key. A car key. The matching car was awaiting collection by its new owner in the hall of the MMC studios. Michaela's ticket number had indeed won the main prize in last night's draw.

And all that had happened without the press getting wind of it! It was almost spooky, because Michaela's most secret wish was that should she ever win something big, no one would come to know of it. She doesn't like to have such things shouted from the rooftops.

The situation was kind of *surreal*. When we entered the hall, workmen were already busy dismantling the gala furnishings. And in the midst of all the busy activity stood our car: lonely, abandoned, and almost forgotten. No one took any notice of us as we walked over to the car. No questions were asked; everyone was absorbed in what they were doing.

We pulled out the key; it fitted. With pounding hearts we started the car. The motor purred divinely. Michaela couldn't believe her luck. We stuffed all the congratulatory balloons into the car and drove unnoticed out of the hall, past the workmen and their machines, and through the greatest commotion. Michaela felt profoundly grateful and accepted by the Universe.

A few days later, we received the car documents. By the way, we have been driving that car ever since, and at the moment it is our only vehicle.

So, once more our wish had been fulfilled in the most wonderful way. We were delighted. Of course, who wouldn't be? Strictly speaking, however, we had simply drawn what had manifested into our lives by wishing for it. Incredible, yet so simple.

Just hand over the problems

Thanking has an additional advantage. By thanking, you confirm that you have definitively handed over the search for a solution to your problem.

That is the wonderful thing about *successful wishing* – that we can simply hand over our worries and problems to 'others' and confirm this by giving thanks.

"Dear Cosmos, dear Angel, dear God or whoever has competence in these matters, please take care of this issue and let me know when it's my turn to take action.

But I do expect clear signs – because I'm now doing what pleases you most. I'm having a great time. I thank you for your help."

From that moment on, we no longer need to occupy ourselves with our problem. Doing so would mean that we are lacking faith in those who we have engaged to take care of it. When we have truly handed over our problems, we know that someone is busy solving them and we can go back to enjoying our day.

> Just hand over your problems
> instead of poring over them.

This is precisely what I have been doing with my worries for years. I simply hand them over. I don't brood on them; I no longer constantly talk about them to myself or in thought to others; I've stopped contemplating variants and alternatives; I don't turn problems over and over in my mind; I've quit trying to force a rational solution. I simply hand them over. And I only take action when I feel an impulse to do so. And – lo and behold – it is usually the right one.

Handing over problems is, incidentally, one of those things I had the opportunity to learn.

The time my girlfriend left me overnight

Many, many years ago I was – totally unexpectedly – plunged into despair. My then girlfriend, with whom I had been living for five years, had met another man. She wanted to be with him. She spent all her days and nights with him, and I found myself in a state of profound unhappiness. I stopped eating and couldn't sleep properly anymore out of sheer lovesickness. It was 'heartrending'. I cried, I raged, I became desperate.

Furthermore, the press reported extensively on the new couple's love-filled bliss and depicted me as the loser, superfluous and only disturbing the idyll of new love.

Inwardly deeply wounded and publicly humiliated, I hit rock bottom.

A week later, I came across a book containing, among other things, the following prayer:

> Lord, grant me the serenity
> to accept the things
> I cannot change,
> the courage to change
> the things I can,
> and the wisdom
> to know the difference.

I read it rather casually. How could a prayer help me in *my* situation?!

The next morning, after ten days of the deepest despair, I said the prayer in thought to myself. In my exhaustion there was nothing to hold on to, nothing to fight for. My girlfriend wanted to live with this other man, and there was nothing to be done about it.

I gave up. I was beaten. I surrendered totally.

Then the words I had been speaking thoughtlessly suddenly began to develop a life of their own. I was inspired. As if someone had switched on a light, I was fulfilled, suffused with a deep feeling of trust. I began to dance and sing in my flat, to cook myself a meal. In my deepest unhappiness I was happy. This experience of happiness was so overwhelming that my eyes repeatedly flowed with tears of joy.

This state of being lasted almost a year. Steeped in bliss, I experienced the world in a completely new and different way. Suffused with the feeling of being carried, with the sense of connection with the Universe or God or my higher self – or whatever you want to call it – I was happy through and through.

My girlfriend came back to me. She felt the power that was emanating from me. But I didn't feel the love for her that I once had. I felt care and respect. I learned to forgive and to acknowledge my own mistakes. Above all, though, I learned to allow my love for myself and to let it flow through everything I did.

The press offered to give my side of the story extensive coverage; they offered to rehabilitate me, but suddenly that wasn't important to me anymore. I was happy and fulfilled. No, public opinion no longer mattered to me. Those who wanted to see the truth would see it. My mind would doubtlessly have said something else, but I consulted my feelings, my intuition, and I have fared very well indeed since.

It wasn't until much later that I realized what had triggered my feeling of happiness: I had quite simply handed over my worries. The whole weight had fallen from my shoulders. From that moment on, I was free to shape my life anew without any constraints. I could enjoy my life. There was nothing that I had to force. After all, I was being taken care of.

Why bother about something that you can't change anyway? That's just love's labor's lost and a waste of energy. I could now utilize all my energy to create beauty in my life.

This experience taught me that most problems are – remarkably enough – only problematic in our mind. Virtually always, what I at first perceived as negative later turned out to be in my best interests.

Whether I had missed a tram, refused a script or been rejected by my partner – all these clouds had a silver lining and led me to a fantastic new 'miracle'.

Everything happens in my best interests.

That is the deep inner knowing that I've had since then. All the unpleasant, 'negative' things are merely corrections that lead me back to my path to happiness.

My love drama set me free for another partner, and made it possible for me to meet Michaela, the greatest joy in my life.

"If you think you can do a thing or
think you can't do a thing,
you're right."

Henry Ford

The **Desire Code**:

Key 4 – Convince the mind

During our childhood, we learned the quickest way of getting a wish fulfilled: beg, whine and scream until we finally get that lollipop.

With wishing it's exactly the other way round. We don't beg, we don't draw attention to everything we lack and how unhappy we are because of this – quite the contrary.

We know
that we will receive what we wish for,
that we are entitled to it and
that it is always available to us.

To most of us, that means changing our way of thinking. How come everything is always available to us? Why does wishing work at all?

So far I have been picturing the Universe as a gigantic online shop. Let's now look more closely at the underlying physical mechanisms, so that even our mind will be convinced that our wishes do indeed manifest.

Don't worry, it's not difficult – just exciting. Most of it will be familiar from physics lessons at school (back then, it may have seemed dry theory of no relevance to our lives). Now these facts are enjoying a new lease of life. Interconnected, they reveal a completely new view of reality.

So, be brave – and embark on this journey into the realm of the unseen. This journey is essential in rendering the notion of *successful wishing* 'comprehensible' to our mind, and thus enlisting its support for our future endeavors.

A bit of physics

Everything is energy. There is nothing but energy. Matter, too, is pure energy. We human beings also consist entirely of energy. Likewise, thoughts, feelings, emotions, events and situations are simply various manifestations of energy.

What does matter consist of, then? Tiny little particles we call atoms. Objects basically differ only in that they are built of different atoms arranged in different ways. All matter in this world is made up of atoms. Atoms join with other atoms, form larger combinations or separate again.

Atoms can be split up into even smaller elementary particles, basically protons, neutrons and electrons. In simplified terms we can imagine this as follows: between the nucleus of the atom (consisting of the protons and neutrons) and the electrons that move around it in circular orbits, there is a lot of empty space.

Incredible but true: if the nucleus of an atom were the size of a pea, the electron shell would be 186 yards (170 meters) away. Most of what we 'see', therefore, is actually emptiness. Yet we perceive it as matter. However, that is merely the way we perceive it; in reality it is not so.

Nothing is as we see it.

We simply absorb the various vibrations and process this information in our brains into an image of matter. We 'translate' it, as it were. Since almost all people translate very similarly (at least that is what we assume), we 'see' and 'feel' things very similarly as well.

Colors, for example, do not exist in reality at all as we perceive them. Vibrations reach our eyes, are converted into electrical impulses and our brain produces the image that we 'see'. The different color frequencies in fact evoke feelings within us; they cause something in us to resonate. That is why we perceive certain colors as feeling cold or warm, despite the material being of the same temperature.

So, everything consists of atoms, which in turn are made up of elementary particles and the latter are an enormous accumulation of energy. Every object on this earth, every human being and every situation is merely a manifestation of energy in various forms. It's only when we grasp this that we are able to understand how we can influence matter.

In 1933, the physicists Marie and Pierre Curie observed how matter can be created out of 'nothing'. They made the scientific discovery that energy can be transformed into matter.

This is where – for our purposes of *successful wishing* – an extremely important element comes into play. Energy can be guided – using the power of our thoughts. Our thoughts are like a laser gun, whose energy beam can be focused on one point. In just the same way, the power of our thoughts guides the energy that is always available everywhere, causing it to condense in a specific form.

Nothing is as we see it. Matter is energy, is created from energy and is kept in its form by energy. There is no matter without energy. Energy can be guided. Each thought is pure energy and in turn affects the energy.

If energy gives rise to matter and thoughts are pure energy, then there are constantly things coming into being around us that we are materializing. After all, we are constantly thinking. To now specifically draw our wishes into our lives, it suffices that we:

Utilize the power of our thoughts.

Ensure that we are resonating with the object of our wishes.

For this purpose we shall harness two laws.

1. The law of conservation of energy

There exists a fundamental law of physics, on which our whole lives are based. It states, as we have already heard, that all material manifestations consist of energy and can be transformed into a different physical form. However, it further states that energy cannot be lost, only transformed. Energy can change and transform, but it can never dissolve 'into thin air'.

The natural philosopher Democritus (460-371 B.C.) discovered that nothing in this world can truly disappear; it always merely changes form. This theory is the foundation of modern physics.

What implications does this have for the *Desire Code*, our *successful wishing*? Just as matter can change into different forms or into energy (which we can't see), energy that is initially invisible can transform into visible matter. And we have the ability to influence this transformation process.

It is always just energy from which new forms of matter arise. Energy is steered and held by consciousness.

What we think, materializes.

That idea can also relate to something *seemingly* impossible – like winning two cars within one year, finding the love of one's life, the right job, the ideal home or perhaps just a second-hand washing machine.

Every wish, thought and idea is 'directed energy'. It is sent out and wants to materialize. In other words, it wants to change into 'matter'. The more intense the thoughts contained in the wish, the more powerful the energy is. The stronger the emotional charge of those thoughts, the greater their impetus.

This unfortunately applies also in the negative sense. Negative thoughts want to become matter, too. Energy doesn't care about what we are thinking. It doesn't distinguish between good and bad; it has no moral principles and doesn't judge. Energy is equally happy to take on any form. It simply switches between forms, subject to the fundamental principle:

> Energy always follows attention.

When we are unhappy, we very often send out negative thoughts into the Universe.

"I'm so unhappy." "I feel so down." "No one loves me." "I'm deplorable." "Everything's hopeless." All these are – in energy terms – commands to the Universe – and will exacerbate our unhappiness.

The same principle, however, can be made to work to our advantage. The thought energy is sent out and condenses. Different energies come together, people tune into them, take them for their own ideas, tinker and work on them a bit, and suddenly the desired partner, the hoped-for event or the longed-for object appears on the doorstep. And it's all just a form of energy.

Strictly speaking, there is an abundant supply of everything in our world. It's entirely a question of distribution. For everyone. For you, too!

Depending on what we *demand*, in energy terms, the *supply* is distributed or constructed in such a way that it enters our lives.

If we live in a world of lack, that lack is by our own order. What we receive is the experience of lack, while our neighbor may be wallowing in wealth, because he has quite simply asked for wealth in his life.

Once we have understood that there is an infinite amount of everything and that our reality aligns with what we ask for, our lives will take shape in a completely different way. After all, energy can take on any form.

There is an abundance of everything,
but it's distributed according to demand.

Wishing is nothing other than a gigantic energy exchange system. Wanted – found. We give energy; we receive energy. We construct our world as it is in our imagination. We shape, we condense, we obstruct or destroy. Energy is always there, and we can shape it according to our will or draw it toward us in a form consistent with our wish.

This is where the law of resonance comes into play.

2. The law of resonance

This states that like always attracts like, whereas unlike things repel each other. Like things, in fact, amplify each other. They resonate. As we know from the piano: when we strike a string, all identically tuned strings start to vibrate too, while strings that are tuned to a different frequency remain totally unaffected.

Our thoughts are likewise energies that vibrate at a very specific frequency. Whatever we are thinking, therefore, sets things that vibrate at that particular frequency in motion.

This also works the other way round, of course. Everything out there in the world that vibrates at the same frequency as our thoughts sets us in motion. Our thoughts are like invisible magnets, attracting everything that is similar to them.

Why do exactly those who already have the most get even more? Because that's the way they think. Because in the world of their thoughts, nothing else exists. Because they live in the resonance field of wealth.

Success attracts more success,
adversity always more and more adversity.

When we're in love, our bliss is complemented by everything else in life also going better. Naturally, because we view the world through positive eyes, positive thoughts create a positive world. We seem to succeed at everything we do.

Our statements now run: "I'm so happy." "The whole world is lying at my feet." "Everything's going just fine."

And sure enough – the world is indeed lying at our feet, because the Universe picks these statements up and processes them.

However, the moment we change our mind and no longer feel carried by love, our outlook on the world becomes more critical and our wish statements run very differently. "He doesn't love me." "I'm sure she's two-timing me." "No one can really love me anyway." "I'm not beautiful." "I feel small and ugly." "The whole world is against me."

And, in a short space of time, our experiences will change completely to correspond with the change in our wish statements. We get a confirmation of our thoughts, without knowing that we are in fact causing these manifestations ourselves. If we were to observe ourselves for a day, we would discover how many such commands we are stating inwardly practically all the time.

Vibrations are vibrations, and they resonate with our thoughts and attitudes. This of course applies to all areas of life. Whether positive or negative.

When something vibrates at a totally different frequency from ours, we do not perceive it at all. Which is not to say, however, that other people do not perceive it either, or that it doesn't exist altogether.

And some biology, too

'Seeing is believing' and 'energy, vibrations – you must show me all those things first' are favorite mantras of staunch 'realists'. The joke is that they are actually proud of them. Why that is a joke and what explanation we can offer our mind when it occasionally unsettles us with such sayings we shall see during an excursion into biology.

The fact is that we can perceive only the smallest part of the truth that surrounds us with our sensory organs. With our eyes, for example, we can see a mere 8 percent of the existing light spectrum.

We cannot recognize the truth.

That is to say, 92 percent of reality escapes our eyes. And our other sensory organs do even more poorly.

Although we are aware that this imperceptible 92 percent exists, we act as if it was totally non-existent – simply because we cannot perceive it. We therefore trust our perception more than actual reality.

The German word for perception, *Wahrnehmung*, derives from *wahr* (true) and *nehmen* (to take). In other words, in German – and in several other languages which use the same construction – perceiving has the essence of "taking in the truth with one's senses".

Let's get one thing straight: our perception is not as 'true' as we may think. The following story illustrates this well. Several blind people are feeling an elephant. The person who is feeling a leg says, "An elephant is round and hard". Another, feeling the trunk, says, "An elephant is thin and constantly flies back and forth".

In exactly the same way we form our image of reality; we take what little we perceive, turn that into an image of our own and are convinced that it is reality.

And by which criteria do we form that image? On the basis of what we already know!

How about the things that we can – thanks to our senses – at least *detect*? How do we deal, then, with the 'mere' 8 percent that we are able to perceive? Do we really absorb all of it?

What we do not 'perceive' does not exist for us.

Even though they constitute only 8 percent of reality as a whole, there exist nonetheless millions of different stimuli every day.

Notes, sounds, images, thoughts, conversations, music, noise – we react to danger, emotions, hustle and bustle, speed; we answer letters, emails, phone calls; we make decisions on behalf of ourselves and others; we read books, gossip magazines, specialist magazines; we're bombarded with advertising; we experience disappointments and rejections and interact with other people.

Every day, we have to process information about information. Only in the fewest cases can we actually think about it. Thinking about something means that we have to take time for it. But it's precisely time that we have only a limited supply of.

For this reason, the mind can't and won't process everything – it simply lacks the capacity to do so.

So it simply switches off in the face of many things – mainly things it already knows and trusts. Why should it raise alarm at the sight of every approaching car? Most of what we are already familiar with is, therefore, quite naturally and subconsciously filtered out of our perception, leaving us enough time for what we consider to be important.

For example, when we are standing at a bus stop, we will certainly not be able to say later on how many cars drove past. That fact was simply not of sufficient importance to pay attention to. The same holds for the people boarding and alighting at the various stops, or the number of pedestrians crossing at the last set of traffic lights.

Perhaps we had been focusing our perception on our newspaper, or we were, in our mind, still with our partner or already at the upcoming meeting at the office.

We always perceive only a small part
of the ascertainable world consciously.

Namely, that part that we consider important and right for ourselves. Subconsciously, we record some *11,000 impressions* per second and store them away in our brain without being aware of it. Only *nine impressions* per second are perceived consciously. This means that our subconscious stores countless things that we are unaware of. Consciously, we perceive only one thousandth of all the things flooding us.

Of the 8 percent of all reality within our scope of perception, we perceive only a thousandth consciously and regard it as being the all-encompassing truth.

The reality we experience is insignificantly tiny compared with the reality that actually surrounds us. We cannot perceive the world in its total fullness. Every day, we decide thousands of times – consciously and, in most cases, subconsciously – where we focus our awareness. Everything else does not exist for us. In fact, if we filter certain things out of our lives for long enough, we cease to believe that these things can exist for others.

But the truth is not the truth! That is merely the mind's attempt to craft an image out of tiny mosaic pieces. It ignores the thousand other mosaic pieces that are also lying around because they don't fit into the picture. In this way it confirms to itself that its perception is correct, and gives us the impression that nothing exists other than what we experience.

"I have not the smallest molecule of faith in aerial navigation other than ballooning or of expectation of good results from any of the trials we hear of."

(Lord Kelvin, mathematical physicist and engineer, 1896)

But how do we set about creating a multifaceted image and living in a more colorful reality that offers us more opportunities? How do we invite a different reality into our lives?

The first step is to acknowledge that there is indeed more than we have previously been aware of. New, unknown things are absorbed into the deeper layers of the mind only when it has heard or read them at least three times. It is therefore good and important for the mind to read this chapter frequently. This helps the mind to free itself from its habitual thought patterns.

The second step is to focus our attention on the desired areas of reality. In order for new and different things to come about in our lives, we must cause different thoughts to vibrate.

Raising our vibrational frequency

This is like changing stations on the radio. We 'tune in' at our own vibrational frequency, through which we let things into our lives. But how do we do that?

We can, for example, raise our frequency by thinking of beautiful things or intonating sacred names. Just singing the sacred word 'Om' or repeating positive affirmations lifts our frequency into previously unknown ranges, and allows what seems unattainable in the material world to enter our lives.

Similarly, positive thoughts have a higher vibrational frequency than negative thoughts. Sending out positive wishes is like turning the radio button. We become more alert to the things that previously hadn't existed in our lives, but that had been floating about on offer 'out there' just the same.

To the extent that if you do not tune in to the desired frequency, you cannot perceive it. You can neither hear it, touch it nor invite it into your bed. If you would like to *wish successfully*, then you must embrace new things, otherwise you cannot perceive them.

It's a fact that when we hold something in our consciousness for long enough, it is compelled to manifest in the material world. Unfortunately, however, our conscious mind is not the only authority that is regularly sending out energy. We have inside us a far more persevering entity that is likewise constantly expressing wishes.

And therefore we shall now address the following question:

What exactly do we constantly and repeatedly
hold in our subconscious?

What are we using to subconsciously filter our wishes? Do we have an inner 'critic'?

Beliefs

The non-manifestation of a wish usually implies the presence of another – stronger – wish. This second wish is then definitely contradicting the first wish, with a longer-lasting impact and considerably greater conviction.

Let's take a look at how we usually set about wishing. On closer observation of our wishing practice, we realize that we spend perhaps ten minutes a day focusing on our wish. We affirm it, we may see it in our mind's eye (in other words, visualize it) and then we return to our everyday lives.

During the remaining 23 hours and 50 minutes, however, we believe that it doesn't work anyway, that it's all nonsense and that strictly speaking we don't deserve to have our wish fulfilled. We're the losers; it's always only the others who have good luck.

Which wish do you think has more power? Which wish do you think has a longer-lasting impact?

The thoughts in our conscious mind and the beliefs in our subconscious mind are often very different or even contrary. Even when the manifestation of the wish is within reach, we cannot make anything of the gift, and let the opportunity pass by.

What is going on here is that we are intensively wishing for something, but on an inner level we are simply not ready to receive it yet. Our desire is leading in a certain direction, but in reality we are not at all capable of actually taking on the new role our desire entails.

That was my own experience, at any rate.

Years ahead of my own evolution

Twenty years ago I already had a deep desire to write. But what? Who would be interested in what I had to say? I didn't know, then, what I should write about and for whom. But I did have the wish. Clear and distinct. I wanted a book written by me to be published. I stated the wish, gave thanks and trusted.

Some weeks later, late at night, I was standing at the bar of a disco in Berlin. Out of the blue, a man turned to me and addressed me: "You are going to write. And you will be writing for me." I didn't understand what this person wanted from me and simply laughed. He, however, remained quite unperturbed: "You are going to write something that only you can write. And I shall publish it."

He handed me his card. He was indeed a publisher – and at one of the largest publishing houses, too – and entering what became a bidding war with other publishing houses.

"But you don't even know whether I can write," I answered. "Or whether I actually want to write at all."

"Would I have spoken to you otherwise?" he inquired with a smile. "You are going to write something, and something very profound at that. When you're ready, give me a call."

I was shocked. My wish had been fulfilled. Without having written a single line, I already had a publisher.

But I was absolutely not ready for it yet. Out of sheer fear that I wouldn't be good enough, of course I didn't call him.

Instead, I had enormous trouble with my girlfriend. She burst into tears, because I had finally found my vocation and she hadn't. For several weeks, she besieged me with her envy and jealousy, and I languished in my feelings of inferiority.

So, the fulfillment of my wish had brought me nothing but trouble. Instead of seizing the opportunity, I crawled into a hole where I did have success, on the stage, where I spoke lines written by others. At the same time, I had the shattering feeling of not having seized the occasion. I felt like a miserable failure.

And all this had happened because I had wished for something that I couldn't handle at all yet.

My wish had manifested, but I couldn't seize the opportunity, because deep down inside me entirely different beliefs were running the show.

"I can't write. No one will take any interest in it. I'll just be making myself ridiculous. I'm a big mouth. I'm a charlatan. If I really show myself, everyone will see that I'm not good enough."

The world is created by the power of thought. Continually, over and over again. Every day and every night.

What we think, we become.

All we have to do, therefore, is to examine what we are thinking. What mental programs are we really running so that our lives are evolving in the way that we are currently experiencing? It's not always that easy to track down all our own programming, as most of it runs quite subconsciously.

What kind of programs are we dealing with here? The easiest way to recognize them is from our opinions on and attitudes to life. The most powerful programs operate through our beliefs. What belief patterns do we have?

Recognizing belief patterns

Since our childhood, we have been filtering countless things out of our lives. We adopt the ideas of our parents and grandparents, our siblings and teachers. We grow up in their world. Everything we have learned from them, the way they treated us, what they said to us and of course how they cared for themselves and interacted with others, how they solved problems, how they managed their relationships and how they faced the world – all that has molded us intensively.

Without questioning these things or examining their degree of truthfulness, we have taken them on board for ourselves.

Since then we have been restricting our perception to the things we believe. And because only that which we see is true for us, we feel reinforced in our beliefs.

"What I believe becomes reality. What I do not believe cannot happen in my life." The fact is that, through our beliefs, we cut ourselves off from the abundance of life.

Belief statements are commands.

We live in a cycle of continually repeating events, because we are permanently creating them through our limiting thoughts. We construct our world according to our beliefs. We feel reinforced in our beliefs and think even more intensely in this direction. That in which we believe will manifest for us.

We could also think quite differently, though. Then quite different things would materialize in our lives. It is, however, not always easy to change our way of thinking. Many of our beliefs are so ingrained in us that it's often difficult to get rid of them or to change them. In most cases it is even difficult to recognize them at all. But a very useful tool is available.

Before you read any further, take a moment to check off the statements below that could have come from you. Which of them do you say about yourself? Which statements did you take on board from your parents, siblings, teachers, friends or the media?

I'm not fit for anything.

I'm not entitled to that.

I'll never be happy.

Who on earth would like me?

I can't accomplish that.

Others are better than I am.

Sex is bad.

Love is always taken advantage of.

True love doesn't exist.

Those who love get deceived.

I never have (enough) money.

Others are better in bed than I am.

I don't think this is going to work out.

I'll never be able to do it right.

Love must be earned.

I don't count anyway.

But what can I change?

It's better to give in than to fight.

I'm going to lose out again.

The way I really am, no one can possibly like me.

I never get what I want, so what's the point?

If I show myself as I really am, everyone will abandon me.

I should be ashamed of myself.

Everything would be alright if...

Friendship and money don't go together.

I shouldn't...

It's all my fault.

No one listens to me anyway.

I don't understand women.

I don't understand men.

No one cares about me.

I can't dance.

I'm bad at math.

I mess everything up.

Others have better sex than I do.

I can't really satisfy a man.

I can't really satisfy a woman.

I'll never make anything of my life.

I always have bad luck.

It's not good to talk about sex.

I'm continually lying to myself.

I don't trust anyone anymore.

I can't trust myself anymore.

Masturbation is a no-no.

Life is hard.

Work is strenuous.

Hard work is the only way to earn money.

Money spoils one's character.

I have a memory like a sieve.

My thinking works too slowly.

I have nothing to say.

No one pays attention to me.

No one can possibly love me.

I can't live without a partner.

I can't relax.

Nothing meets my expectations.

Love makes you vulnerable.

Love passes.

When I want something, I always have to work for it.

I always get used by others.

No pain, no gain.

Self-praise stinks.

I can't do that.

He doesn't deserve me.

I must first pay off my debts.

I must not have such wishes.

I feel small and ugly.

The whole world is against me.

There are no miracles in my life.

My work is worthless.

There is never enough.

I'm not good enough.

No one loves me.

We also have self-definitions in the form of "I am" expressions. By the way, 'definition' literally means the demarcation or marking out of a boundary. When we self-define, we mark boundaries around our beliefs and shut out the rest of reality.

I'm insignificant.

I'm lonely.

I'm stupid.

I'm helpless.

I'm worthless.

I'm useless.

I'm just a burden.

I'm too good for this world.

I'm guilty.

I'm bad.

I'm anxious.

I'm not musical.

I'm lazy.

I'm ill.

I'm too fat.

I'm too thin.

I'm too small.

I'm not clever enough.

I'm a bad person.

I'm shy.

I'm too serious.

I'm not serious enough.

I'm happy being single.

I'm immature.

I'm not erotic.

I'm conservative.

I'm down-to-earth.

I'm addicted to sex.

I'm not sexy.

I'm not articulate.

I'm impotent.

I'm frigid.

I'm perverse.

I'm not normal.

I'm easily seduced.

I'm weak.

I'm unimaginative.

I'm arrogant.

I'm hard, but fair.

I'm scatterbrained.

I'm different than others.

I'm humorless.

I'm not talkative.

I'm an idiot.

I'm too old.

I'm not lovable.

I'm selfish.

I'm not important enough.

I'm always so tired.

I'm clumsy.

I'm not beautiful.

I'm constantly ill.

I'm unhappy.

Which of these beliefs apply to you?

With which do you identify?

Which of them has become second nature to you to such a degree that you regard them as your truth?

It's safe to assume that you have checked off several statements. Well, now you know what wishes you are constantly sending out without being aware of it. Often these subconscious wishes act as a brake on our conscious wishes or reverse them altogether.

Beliefs are incredibly powerful wishes.

They are thought or spoken with tireless constancy. For example, if you believe that you must earn love, you are constantly sending this out and it will be just as constantly fulfilled. If you believe that the only way of obtaining money is through hard work, then that will be your experience.

From this mixture of different beliefs, we put together our personality. Everything that lies beyond our personal beliefs, we subconsciously fight against.

When we want to think *new* thoughts and form *different* beliefs, however, and send those out into the world, we don't need to repeat them a thousand times in order to cancel the old thoughts. No, energy reacts faster than we would deem possible.

Nevertheless, we may perhaps take some time to become convinced by the new belief statements and might, consequently, transmit a great deal of doubt simultaneously with the wish.

And hence a strange medley of wishes reaches our Universal 'account manager'. Which one has priority? Obviously the one that can look back on a long history. Every other account manager in this world would probably proceed similarly. He would check the old files and then base his decision on the extent to which the wish corresponds to our habits.

Many wishes are formulated from a consciousness of lack.

If, for example, my wish runs: "I am beautiful," then it hardly serves my purpose if I do not truly believe that. If I spend ten minutes a day consciously realizing my wish, and the remaining 23 hours and 50 minutes being convinced of the contrary, which wish is going to manifest?

Resolving belief patterns

So, how can we set about resolving old belief patterns? By recognizing where they really belong, and when and why they arose.

The best thing to do is to write down all the items you marked on the list on a sheet of paper, and to think about where these convictions actually come from. When and where did they arise? What events led to their existence? Whose stock phrases were these statements? Which people held these convictions about themselves? And who led us to believe over and over again that we exhibit this particular behavior?

When we go back there again, when we go back to the source, we will discover the truth.

> *Sit down in a quiet and comfortable place, and pick one of the items you marked on the list. Close your eyes and repeatedly ask yourself: "Where did all this start?"*

> *You will be astonished at the long-forgotten images that come up. Things that happened what seems like a long time ago, but that still shape your self-image today.*

> *And suddenly we realize that many of our convictions in fact aren't ours at all, but originate from our father or mother. Perhaps they're statements that our parents were forever preaching to us. At some point we took these on board as applying to ourselves. We began to identify with them. From childhood we have been carrying these false belief patterns around with us.*

> *The beliefs instilled in us by another person's preaching are not the only valid truth. Once we acknowledge that, our attitude to ourselves will change. We will see ourselves with different eyes. No longer will we be so convinced of our previous self-image – and that is a good thing. It takes the wind out of the sails of our negative commands to the Universe.*

The goal of this exercise is to weaken the negative commands and strengthen the positive ones. This occurs gradually. Spaces are emptied and start to fill with new content – and that's the reason why we should start working actively on our list of positive wishes parallel to putting the brakes on our negative beliefs. Miracles happen through positive beliefs.

As we recall: matter arises from energy and is shaped by focused energy. Whatever we think, manifests.

To the energy, it doesn't matter what we are wishing for. It simply works for or against us, according to our expectations.

- We limit ourselves by our thoughts.

- We limit ourselves by our beliefs.

- We limit ourselves by negative commands.

- We only ever experience that which we believe.

- Everything is possible if we consider it possible.

Let's take the example of wishing to be more attractive. How do we set about convincing ourselves that we are beautiful?

Beauty exercise

Choose a quiet moment, switch off the phone and find a place in your home where you will not be disturbed for some time. A pleasant soft light would be welcome, and we require a large mirror – perhaps from the hall or from the bathroom.

And then sit down in front of this large mirror, preferably naked. What normally happens? We immediately see all our physical faults. Too fat, too soft, too flabby, too droopy, too old, too big, too small, too light, too wrinkly, too shapeless. We usually focus instantly only on our cellulite, on our bumps and dents and skin blemishes.

When someone tells us how beautiful we are, we fend them off vehemently, and – promptly and with remarkable readiness – point out what isn't okay about our body. Isn't it amazing? We all want to be beautiful, but when someone actually sees beauty in us, we immediately convince them of the contrary and quite openly show them our defects, which we would in fact like to conceal.

In this way, however, not only do we convince the other person of our ugliness, but we also convince ourselves – constantly.

We are our own greatest critics.

We relent only when the other person realizes their 'mistake'. No, of course we're not beautiful! Our task of convincing ourselves and others accomplished, we usually tumble into deep sadness. Not being beautiful would be particularly unpleasant – and yet we convince ourselves and others of it every day.

Let's return to ourselves and the mirror in front of which we are sitting. Today we shall do this differently. Today we shall view ourselves in a completely calm and relaxed way – without passing judgment. We observe our breathing, our skin, our joints. We feel the warmth and intimacy of the moment. This is our body, which does such a good job. Every day, every minute, it is there for us. Never does it give up – no matter how much we ill-treat and exert it. No matter how much we insult and ignore it. Our body is wonderful. Without it, we could not experience all those delightful things.

We spend a few minutes paying our body due regard for its tireless efforts. We feel the gratitude that we have for our body.

After a while we shift our focus to what we like about our body. That could be our hair, our mouth, our shoulders, a finger, our big toe, our breasts or our backside. Perhaps it is 'only' our navel. There will always be something that we like – and on that we shall now focus, while observing that:

"I am open and ready for my wish for beauty to manifest now. I am now able to allow this miracle into my life. I know that the negative thoughts do not belong to me, and that they are getting weaker and weaker every day. I love my body and view it with great admiration. I am beautiful and desirable – and I am entitled to be so."

If we repeat this for several evenings running, treating ourselves and our body with this degree of respect, we will discover more and more parts of our body that we are pleased with. Every day, we will embrace ourselves more. Our body is beautiful and wonderful. It puts in a tremendous amount of work and, now that we are showing it respect and acknowledgment, it is starting to become more beautiful every day.

That is not to say that our body will immediately change and become more beautiful (as if there were such a thing as an ugly body!), but our self-image changes. We no longer apply an unnatural benchmark and say: "Only when my body looks like that of Claudia Schiffer or Brad Pitt will it be beautiful." We see the beauty of our body *now*. Inner beauty attracts outer beauty – and because of this, our body will indeed become more and more beautiful, and our charisma will increase.

If we send the wish "I am beautiful" out now, our secret resistance will have decreased considerably. The wish can finally manifest.

I allow beauty in.

We take ourselves more and more into the vibrational frequency of beauty. We send this energy out, and simultaneously raise the frequency of our own vibrations. The law of conservation of energy and the law of resonance are working for us.

Perhaps just a short time later, someone will come up to us and tell us how beautiful we are. And this time we will not make the mistake of trying to convince them of the contrary. "Yes, I am beautiful. And I become more and more beautiful every day."

Impossible? No, nothing is impossible. Here's yet another example that nothing is impossible – as long as we believe it is possible. Sometimes we just have to stop telling ourselves over and over again why something cannot work out. Sometimes we are outright looking for reasons to fail.

Besides, some wishes are delivered immediately. We must merely keep in mind that, through our own conscious and subconscious beliefs, we are the creators of our own lives.

The impossible is carried out immediately

When we were working in Munich on the final cut of our film, *And That's Just the Beginning*, we felt so at home that we absolutely wanted to move back to Munich. The weather was beautiful, the people were friendly and all our friends were there again. Munich was simply our home.

But immediately thousands of limiting beliefs popped up, arguing why this definitely couldn't work.

It's not that easy to return to our native town, because our daughter Julia is attending an international school in Bonn.

It would be impossible to enroll her at a school in Munich, as all the English-language schools are totally overcrowded.

The waiting lists at these schools run to several years.

Of course we could wish, but reality dictates that our wish would take some time to manifest, and there are only two days left before the summer holidays.

The school offices are probably all empty by now.

The class lists for the next school year have of course been drawn up. Long ago.

There is no place. Not for us, and not for anyone in the whole world.

This year is a no-go. No matter how hard we wish. It probably won't even work out next year either.

At that point we realized that we had fallen into our own trap of limiting beliefs. In other words, we were busy creating our own failure.

We changed course immediately and started wishing the proper way. After all, *successful wishing* had already become more or less second nature to us.

But pursuing the wish did not strike us as particularly realistic.

Why not?

Our minds were at it again, having crept in through the back door with all their doubts.

Why didn't we just go for it and let things take their course?

And strangely enough, no sooner had we formulated and sent the wish, than I felt a persistent urge to phone one of the best international schools in Munich.

Michaela just smiled. Of course it was utter nonsense, said my mind. Of course the manifestation of this wish was a sheer impossibility. Of course there was no way this could work out.

However, after sending out a wish, Michaela always listens very attentively to the subtler energies.

Less than two minutes later she had acted on my impulse and phoned the school management.

The incredible miracle started to take shape. She was told that there was indeed still a place available in the second-year group – another pupil had just been withdrawn – and we were invited to visit the next day, the last day of the school year. We were warned not to entertain too high hopes, though, as a lengthy admissions procedure was normally required.

So the next day we found ourselves, to our amazement, in the headmistress's office. On the way there, we had encountered the parents of a child for whom there was no place; in tears, they told us that this meant they would be moving back to England.

All in all, it was clear to us that, notwithstanding the headmistress's cordiality, our application would be rejected too, like thousands of others each year. Yet we had wished and the wish had led us here. Right into the office of the headmistress, who by some miracle still had one place to offer. The only place in the whole school. And, into the bargain, this place was in the second-year group, in which Julia belonged.

The headmistress spoke at length with Julia and gave her several tests; they conversed intensively in English and then, after an hour, the miracle became reality. The headmistress nodded approvingly at us and entered Julia in the list of new pupils.

If ever anything had been truly impossible, it was this: securing a place at this school within one day. For years afterwards, other parents confirmed to us the sheer incomprehensibility of this miracle.

"There are only two ways to live your life.
One is as though nothing is a miracle.
The other is as though everything
is a miracle."

Albert Einstein

The **Desire Code**:

Key 5 – Have faith instead of doubts

Doubts are another form of belief with a very negative impact on our wishing. A particularly important factor of *successful wishing* is to avoid nourishing your doubts, as to doubt is to believe in the non-fulfillment of one's own wish.

> People who claim not to believe in their wish
> do in fact believe in the opposite of their wish.

We constantly *believe* in **something**, even if we know that that belief holds us back.

Strangely enough, we are better at doubting than we are at practicing our faith in *the Desire Code*.

But by doubting we get in our own way. By doubting we recall our wishes when we have barely sent them out. Often we think or say parallel to our wish, "That's not going to work anyway". This thought, however, is also a pronounced wish. Our expectation is then: "It doesn't work" or "It doesn't work in my life". And what is going to happen then? This sent-out wish is delivered just the same.

Doubt is also a very clear wish

So, if you decide to limit yourself, you will experience precisely this limitation.

Fearful thoughts act as a brake on our wishes, too. Behind the thought, "What on earth am I going to do if that doesn't work out?" lurks doubt. If we were convinced that our wish was going to be fulfilled, we wouldn't need to worry, would we? This worry only goes to show that we are holding on more to our doubts than to the fulfillment.

Many people then say, "I really did wish for it so much, but it never manifested. I knew it all along." But *what* did they know all along? They knew with certainty that wishing doesn't work for them. They sent this knowledge out simultaneously with the wish and thus robbed the wish of all its energy.

What usually happens, therefore, is that the doubts – which are false beliefs –superimpose themselves on the consciously stated wish.

We are always successful.
Usually at creating failure.

All the positive thinking, all the mantras in the world won't help us if deep inside we are continually thinking in terms of lack and limitations.

Doubt is a deeply rooted attitude. It is a firmly anchored belief that materializes just the same.

> He who doesn't believe in success
> cannot have success.

The way out

So, what are we to do with our doubts? With that little voice that keeps saying that we don't deserve something, or that this wishing business doesn't work anyway? How do we manage to avoid listening to it or thinking of it?

That's like not being allowed to think about chocolate when you want to lose weight. You try quite consciously to 'not' think about chocolate, and end up thinking about it more than ever. Not thinking about something is in fact impossible, because the mere attempt at not thinking about it requires you to first establish what it is you don't want to think about.

Avoidance, then, is a bad strategy, because it focuses your thoughts on the very thing you are seeking to avoid.

The best thing to do, then, is to just allow the thoughts and not judge them. They're there, they come bubbling up, we observe them briefly – after all, they're only thoughts and we won't attach any further power or significance to them – and without passing comment on them, we release them and send them on.

New thoughts present themselves, some arising from everyday life, some from our past. They're just thoughts; there's nothing bad about them. It's only when you get annoyed about them that they start to disturb you. Only when you try to prevent them do they gain power. It is only convictions like "I just can't manage it" or "My thoughts keep bothering me and destroying all my wishes" that create this scenario.

Allowing and not passing judgment is therefore the only way. Thoughts come and go and do not disrupt the *successful wishing* process. We trust our wishes. Disturbing thoughts have no power, because we do not give them any power.

We could even go a step further and turn the tables:

> Why always doubt the good things?
> Why not question the bad things?

After all, we could doubt whether the negative thoughts are actually our truth. In this way, doubt can serve as a brake on the constant manifestation of our limiting beliefs.

From my own experience I know, however, how quickly we can succumb to our own negative doubts. Especially when we find ourselves under mounting pressure.

Wishing for the ideal house

When we were planning to move from Bonn to Munich, we had only my small office in Munich. Michaela, being of a very sunny disposition, absolutely wanted to find a wonderful home in the vicinity of my office so that I wouldn't have to struggle through the commuter traffic every day. In fact, she even went a step further. She was convinced that we would be able to rent a beautiful little house, at most three minutes on foot from my office. I was also convinced and so we submitted our wish.

But no matter where we inquired, we met with disbelieving headshakes. The real estate agents we had commissioned soon made it clear to us that we would certainly not find anything within a year. Not in this area. They already had clients living in hotels, simply because there was nothing being offered around here. There was no response to our classified ads in the newspaper. The more intensively we sought, the more impossible the fulfillment of our wish seemed to become.

Four weeks before our planned move to Munich, the moving company started to get nervous. They wanted to know where they were supposed to take our furniture. So did I, actually.

They had to arrange things like parking permits and claim parking space for their van. But our 'wished-for' house was still nowhere in sight – quite the contrary. It was clear to me that this wasn't going to work out. We had pushed our luck too far.

And then the doubts started stirring inside me. More than once I considered renting storage space for our furniture. I was convinced that this time things would go wrong. But Michaela remained unshakable in her faith. "The house will come to us. We've wished for it, so why should we have doubts?" Of course she was right. Of course. But by this time the situation was getting rather serious.

What if the Universe's notion of time differed from ours? Or the Universe had just received a vast number of wishes and was processing them in order of the date of receipt? Was our 'account manager' perhaps busy with entirely different things – substantially more important things than our modest wish for a house in the immediate vicinity of my office?

And what were we to say to the moving people? "We have just submitted a wish to the Universe for a new house and the Universe always delivers in due time"? They would've thought we had gone completely mad.

To be honest, there were moments when I did indeed consider Michaela a bit... well, shall we say, stubborn.

But ultimately our marriage was more important to me than the ever-increasing probability of ending up on the street with our furniture. Actually, the thought of sitting on the sofa between parked cars and drinking coffee was quite amusing. But what would we do if it started to rain?

Every day I became more nervous. Above all, because Michaela – in her boundless innate faith – had dismissed all the estate agents who did not share her belief in a successful outcome (which was all of them). Her attitude was: why should she surround herself with energies that counteracted her wish? So, shortly before we were due to move, we had no house and no one looking for a house on our behalf.

So far I had been exceptionally good at *successful wishing*, but now we had quite clearly come up against our limits. Not as far as Michaela was concerned, though. The deadline was drawing closer and closer. Eventually Michaela would have to face the truth. And the ugly truth was so obvious. This time the prompt delivery hadn't worked out. Our furniture would be dumped on the street.

However – to my incomprehension – Michaela refused to face this truth. She saw no reason to doubt. On the contrary, she encouraged me to not give further room to my own doubts and to confidently hold on to the manifestation of our wish.

And then the miracle actually happened. It began quite inconspicuously in a pharmacy. The pharmacist recognized us. Many years ago, she had sold us a pregnancy test and, two hours later, a second one, because the first one hadn't produced a clear result and I had got on Michaela's nerves until she asked the pharmacist for advice. Was the color line on the test strip red or was it blue? She still remembered that very well indeed.

Well, we struck up a conversation, and suddenly she told us that an old friend of hers was moving away and planning to rent his house. Here, just around the corner.

Less than ten minutes later we phoned the owner of the house and set up an appointment to view it the next day. But of course we couldn't wait that long. That afternoon we sneaked around the house and viewed it from the outside. We liked it. It was our house. It felt like our house. But the viewing appointment the next day was for all the other prospective tenants as well. Why should we be the ones to get this house?

"Perhaps because we wished for it and it is now being delivered," smiled Michaela in her unshakeable faith.

And then the second miracle – or the second installment of the delivery – happened.

As we were slowly walking away from the house, an old lady came along and tried to open the garden gate. But it stuck. Although we were a considerable distance away, she called to us and asked us to help her. We opened not only the garden gate for her, but also the front door, and when we said that we would be coming to view the house the next day, she offered to show us around straight away. We thus got a private guided tour of 'our' house.

The house was precisely what we were looking for. We were thrilled. In our mind's eye, we already saw how we would allocate the rooms and which pieces of furniture we would put where.

We weren't there yet, however. The elderly lady didn't want to make a decision in advance but there was a mutual sympathy between us and she wanted to phone her son, who would take care of the contractual arrangements. The next day we met the whole family before the other prospective tenants arrived.

It was a wonderful afternoon, and it was clear to everyone that we would get the house. Although others subsequently offered more money, presumably backed by an income considerably more steady than ours, a short time later we held the tenancy agreement in our hands.

A miracle? Coincidence? Or the delivery of our wish?

There was one major handicap, though. The house would be available in three months' time. It was still fully furnished and there was no possibility of our future landlord moving out sooner.

But even that was no problem. We were allowed to bring all our furniture into the house right away, and until the property became available we would sleep at the office.

Shortly afterwards, however, the family moved out sooner than they had planned, meaning we could move in earlier than we had anticipated – into our wonderful house that had been delivered precisely according to our specifications and schedule.

But things got better still. Not only did the house fulfill our wish in all respects, including the three-minute walk to my office, but the landlords are a true joy to know personally, as are the neighbors. An exceptional stroke of luck.

So Michaela was right after all. The Universe always delivers. So why have doubts?

Doubting is like canceling the wish.

A doubt is like a counter-wish. We countermand the whole order. Our doubts convey the message that this just won't work. The wish then quite simply becomes: "It will go wrong." What the Universe subsequently delivers is a confirmation of our idea that it just won't work.

That would certainly have been my experience had Michaela not remained so steadfast.

Secrecy

A further essential key to *successful wishing* is to not talk about it. Do not talk to anyone about your wish until it has manifested.

First, constantly talking about the wish causes the energy to fall flat. Second, it very quickly attracts the attention of people who oppose, envy or doubt us, and gives room to their beliefs and convictions.

Talking about our own wish weakens it.

Why is this?

All truly great ideas are born in secrecy. Every idea starts out as an impulse, a thought, that disappears again if it is not picked up. At first there is just a vague notion that slowly takes shape and finally – after some time – appears as a clear product or object before the mind's eye. It's only when we have consolidated our own mental picture that greater visions and concrete plans arise from it.

We must first sufficiently strengthen our own structure and our own mental picture before taking them into the outside world in order to secure others' enthusiasm and commitment for our new project.

If we were to do that too soon, we would not be anywhere near steadfast enough. At this stage, just a few disparaging or deprecating words would probably suffice to make us give up the project.

Once we have grown with our own idea and are sufficiently resolute in our new plans, however, our wish has become so concrete that we are able to really champion it – in spite of headwinds and adversaries.

All the world's greatest inventors can confirm this process. Secrecy is of utmost importance – not only because of the risk of plagiarism, but also because it enables us to build up our confidence. Who wants to make a laughing stock of themselves with ideas that don't come to fruition? The next time we will trust our own ideas even less, and eventually we will be so convinced of our inferiority that we won't allow ourselves to have any new ideas or concepts at all.

In the wishing context, a further and completely different aspect comes into play. We fear that others will consider us completely crazy. Who is going to believe something that 'weird'? We're afraid of suddenly being dismissed as cranks and esoteric and not taken seriously.

And who will be making the most fun of us? Those people whose lives are even less in order and who, for that reason, don't want anything to get better in ours. All the things *they* don't believe in should certainly not happen in *our* lives either. It's therefore better to stay silent.

When we have gained sufficient experience and had many a wish fulfilled, we will be happy to inform others about our wishing – because now we are steadfast enough. We are aware of the power of our thoughts. For us, there are no 'coincidences' any more. And our example can serve to inspire and encourage others.

Forgetting

While we're on the subject of staying silent, note that it's best to stay silent towards ourselves, too. In other words, we don't give our wish any further thought; we simply forget it.

Forgetting has several advantages. One is that we subsequently also forget to doubt and to thereby reverse the whole order. Furthermore, by forgetting we demonstrate our faith. We are so sure that what we are wishing for will manifest in our lives that we no longer concern ourselves with it.

After all, others are supposed to be doing that on our behalf. This faith leaves us open to receiving the object of our wish – no matter in what predicament we happen to be right now. In this way we allow ourselves to be guided to the right place at the right time. Just like it happened to me recently.

Amsterdam airport is closed

Successful wishing can be applied in any situation. And, of course, especially when things aren't going particularly well in life. However, precisely in these situations we sometimes forget to wish for something, and frantically try to fight. Yet we can get out of the pointless struggle just as quickly as we fell into it.

An example of this happened to me at Amsterdam airport. Heavy snowfall had caught many people totally unawares and paralyzed the entire airport. During several hours of patient waiting, the snowstorm had become so severe that the whole airport was closed for the night.

The situation was hopeless. The waiting passengers were provided with drinks, blankets and pillows for the night.

Countless people were annoyed, angry, exhausted and quarreling. But their negative attitude to the unalterable situation had not helped them to make the night more pleasant. Thousands stood at the ticket counters; thousands more tried to get access to their luggage, which was stowed in the planes' holds. No one was properly informed and everyone was wandering about helplessly.

I was in much the same situation at first, allowing myself to get caught up in the commotion. After all, the next day I had important appointments, which I now would not be able to keep. I began to sweat in my thick jacket and got carried away in aimless actions.

Suddenly, however, I remembered *successful wishing* again. What can't be changed must be accepted. "Enjoy every moment of your life, keep your spirits up and simply order the best solution to the situation" – which helped on this particular night.

My order was quite simple and ran: "For tonight I have a beautiful and quiet hotel room, and I will obtain the best means of returning to Munich. I am now open and ready for this information."

I gave thanks for the fulfillment of my wish, thereby dispatching it, and was willing to forget the urgency of my situation. I knew that from then on, the best solution for me was being taken care of.

First, I sat down calmly and observed the unusual hubbub. It doesn't happen every day that an airport is closed. There were things to see that I hadn't experienced before. And so I suddenly found myself observing a marvelous spectacle. While countless people quarreled over tickets for the next day – without it being in the least certain that the flights would be able to resume by then – I sat there drinking coffee. I simply knew that the right thing for me would happen.

Although the airport hotel had closed due to overcrowding, as had adjacent hotels, I felt calmer and calmer. People were in despair, children were crying; the situation seemed to be getting more and more hopeless with every minute that passed. The car rental agencies closed, as all their vehicles had been rented. My mind made itself heard and scolded me for not securing a vehicle in time, but my feeling was still one of tranquility. A rented car didn't seem to be the best solution, then.

I got hungry, strolled around, leaned against a counter with a beaker of coffee and observed all the frantic crowds of people. Suddenly a signboard was flipped over, a glass pane was pushed aside and a woman's voice asked me what my destination was.

I had been leaning against a train ticket counter. "Munich," I replied in bewilderment. "7:03 a.m., with one change," said the lady, and before I could give any kind of answer, she slid a ticket across the counter. "You can leave from here early tomorrow morning, or from Amsterdam Central Station."

Without thinking twice I bought the ticket, and when I turned round, I saw that an endless line of people had formed behind me. While I had been leaning against the closed counter, I had been the only person there, and now it was overpopulated; the people at the end of the line would certainly have to wait an hour or longer.

Not having any idea what to do until seven o'clock the next morning, I wandered around, and without any particular purpose I went into the basement. There stood a local train to Amsterdam Central Station. I boarded. In the same moment the train departed. The conductor asked me where I was going to stay overnight, and spontaneously recommended a hotel ten minutes' walk from the station, on a small side street, as all the other hotels were bound to be fully booked on account of the snowfall.

At the station, some thirty to forty people were standing around a taxi and squabbling. I saw travelers with heavy luggage and a bewildered gaze coming out of two station hotels where they had been turned away. Totally calm, I tramped through the snow following the conductor's directions, found the hotel and got the last available room. The very last one that evening. A truly beautiful, large and quiet room. I ordered something to eat, and – to crown a successful evening – even a glass of champagne.

Without having to fight for a place with others in long lines, the best solution for the night had quickly opened up to me – and without a problem.

Now I was curious whether the train would indeed turn out to be the right and fastest option.

Early the next morning, I saw travelers sleeping in the hotel lobby and learned that the airport was still closed, and would probably remain so for the whole day. Some of them had even spent up to four hours waiting in their planes, before having to disembark again, exhausted and disappointed.

On my train to Germany, I encountered travelers who had spent the whole night in the overcrowded station hall, and they told me that those who had managed to get hold of a car during the night had had to turn back after only a few miles as the motorways had been closed, too.

The train was thus indeed not just the *best* but also the *only* means of getting from Amsterdam to Munich on this day.

Without the *successful wishing*, I would probably have spent a terrible night and persevered in vain for much longer at the airport. Instead, I had had a good sleep and was enjoying my breakfast in the dining car, as a white snowy landscape rolled by.

It's up to everyone to decide for themselves, then, whether a situation is indeed awful or whether it's wonderful. Whether it leads to something even worse, or whether it's evolving in the best possible way.

Things are the way they are. Every moment you can choose whether they are working for you or against you. The only decisive factor is always your outlook. My outlook on life is that I always expect the best. And the simplest way to do this is through *successful wishing*.

> "Men often become what they believe themselves to be. If I believe I cannot do something, it makes me incapable of doing it. But when I believe I can, then I acquire the ability to do it even if I didn't have it in the beginning."
>
> Mahatma Ghandi

The **Desire Code**:

Key 6 – Be open to 'coincidences'

It is impossible to figure out in advance how a wish will be delivered because the wish is always fulfilled in a way we would never have considered possible. So, we should simply be prepared to have our wish fulfilled. If we keep looking only in the direction from which we expect the delivery to occur, we may miss it because we're expecting the wish to be delivered exclusively in the exact way that fits into our limited imagination.

The Universe, however, is considerably more resourceful. In cases such as mine in Amsterdam, we like to say that a miracle has happened, because we're taken completely by surprise that there were suddenly so many 'coincidences' in our life that enabled our wish to manifest.

The Universe delivers in surprising ways

What actually happens is simply the manifestation of our wish. And yet this often occurs in a way that we hadn't anticipated. However, this merely says something about our powers of imagination and not about the many possibilities there are of having our wishes fulfilled.

If, for example, we wish for money, then we should leave the way by which the money will find us entirely open. Being convinced that, for example, only Aunt Erna will give us the money we want is a mental deadlock that prevents us from recognizing other possibilities.

The Universe always chooses the fastest and easiest way.

Perhaps Aunt Erna doesn't want to give us the money at all. Then she won't pick up on the intentions sent out by our thoughts. She just doesn't resonate with them. Our dispatched energy therefore doesn't linger with Aunt Erna, but continues to spread out further until it encounters something that resonates at the same frequency and responds.

In other words, our wishing energy isn't out to persuade anyone or anything; it's just a cosmic search engine.

Since we can't know who or what will respond to our wish, we naturally have no idea from which direction the money could arrive. And given that we have no idea, it would be pretty foolish to commit to a certain direction. And yet we do it. Even I constantly catch myself having a predefined idea, and hence not immediately noticing the delivery of my wishes.

"Where is my order?" – or "I'm on the wrong train!"

I often take the train instead of flying. I think I can make better use of my time that way. I usually sit in the dining car for a while, watching a film on my laptop. That was certainly the case this time. In the morning, upon leaving the house, I quickly formulated and sent out my wish. I wanted coffee and cake first, then I wanted to watch a film, and I had everything I needed with me: my laptop and a DVD.

All ICEs (InterCity Express high-speed trains) are equipped with power connectors. But suddenly I found myself on an IC (InterCity train), with no dining car and no power sockets. On top of that, the train was completely overcrowded. The only available seat was at a table, where I sat opposite a couple who stared at me in a friendly manner. Hadn't my order arrived this time? With the train this full, surely it would have been better to sit in a corner rather than in the middle of an open-plan carriage?

At any rate, I was absolutely not satisfied with what the Universe had procured for me and swore under my breath. Suddenly the man sitting opposite me knocked his knee on something and rubbed the sore spot. "A power socket," he muttered morosely to his wife. "Who on earth needs such a thing?"

"I do!" I shrieked inwardly and glanced in amazement under the table – where there was indeed a power socket.

I had electricity for my little cinema. And what's more, this same Swabian couple unpacked a picnic basket. However incredible it may seem, they set the table for themselves and also furnished a cup of coffee for me. With cake. "Because coffee just isn't complete without cake," said the man with a grin, adding that he hoped that I would enjoy my film.

The order had gone out and the Universe had delivered. I had perhaps imagined things somewhat differently, but the delivery had been made promptly. And that's precisely the amusing thing about *successful wishing*. The wishes are always fulfilled; we just have to trust and stay alert – because the way in which the Universe delivers is often surprising.

But how do we manage to avoid missing the delivery?

Intuition

How are our wishes fulfilled? Certainly in a different way than we expect. It's unfortunately not always a matter of imagining something and having it come flying from above onto our table. As everything is a question of energy, we are sometimes guided very subtly – to where the manifestation of our wish is to be found.

But how are we guided?

That can sometimes be a conversation that we happen to overhear for some strange reason and that contains important information for us. Or it can be an apparently random thought that we pursue. Perhaps we suddenly decide to take a different route than usual, and precisely there we 'coincidentally' run into an old acquaintance, who quite 'coincidentally' tells us about someone we should get to know. And, 'strangely enough', that person has exactly what we are wishing for: a new house, a tool for the blocked pipes, or else he knows someone who can fix our computer problem. Or someone bangs his knee and calls our attention to a hidden power connector.

Energy flows, steers, guides, leads. All we have to do is be open to it. After we have sent out our wish, it's simply a matter of staying alert and keeping our ears open. Then we'll get all the information we need – and the surest means is through our intuition.

Intuition – what is that?

Intuition is allowing ourselves.

To get in touch with our intuition, all we have to do is pursue whatever feels good. No matter how strange, embarrassing or ridiculous it may seem in the first instance. Intuition is nothing other than spontaneous action. When something occurs to us that we would like to do, we do it. We don't look for the pros and cons. We don't consider carefully. We follow our impulse.

Intuition is the opposite of reason. We cannot think about it. Intuition is not a logical consequence of in-

127

tensive contemplation – it works through feelings and sensations.

To follow the voice of our intuition, we must let ourselves drift, without fixing our attention on a goal. When we refrain from questioning and judgment; when we pay attention to the still, quiet thoughts and simply follow them; when we stay in the moment instead of staying stuck in the past or squinting into the future, we will come into contact with our intuition.

<blockquote>
The mechanism of one's intuition
unfolds only in the present.
</blockquote>

Our intuition helps us to start acting spontaneously and strengthens our faith in our own perception. Instead of having to face the challenges of everyday life ourselves, we allow ourselves to drift towards the desired solution. What we are in fact doing is again picking up the ethereal energy that we sent out earlier. In returning to us, it guides us to where we will receive the fulfillment of our wish. Put simply, it is our sense of anticipation that is leading us.

Of course we're uncertain of ourselves at first. As with everything, we need a bit of practice and experience. But even though it's initially difficult to recognize how intuition feels, after a short while of engaging it we will have acquired a keen sense of the strong ally at our side. Quite soon we will become a single entity. We are not alone. Never again. Within us there is a higher authority that guides and leads us to the desired answer.

Don't worry, *successful wishing* always works. Even without intuition. But it works considerably faster with intuition. Our intuition is simply like a postal address, to which the Universe sends information about where we can collect what we are wishing for. Although I have often quite consciously acted against my intuition, the delivery was made all the same. Sometimes it just arrived somewhat later.

Here are two small examples of how concretely and directly our intuition works.

Express deliveries

If I want something delivered particularly quickly, I order it by asking questions. "Where can I find what I'm wishing for?" or "What's the fastest way of obtaining ...?" By doing this, I quite consciously instruct the energy that I'm sending out to report back to my intuition.

And then I relax and listen attentively for the slightest sign. Sometimes the answer is a sentence spoken by the person standing next to me in a pub, or a newspaper headline, or the lyrics of a song on the radio.

Many years ago, when I wasn't yet all that familiar with my intuition, I had some difficulty recognizing the signs. Often I didn't know whether I was talking myself into something or whether my mind was quite consciously pushing me in a certain direction.

I remember very well the time when – in spite of my professional success – my loneliness and feeling of emptiness were overwhelming. My deepest wish back then was simply to understand what the purpose of my life was.

I recall sitting in a café in Munich and repeatedly thinking out loud, "What's this crap all about? Where's the purpose in this whole business?" I was really peeved. "I'm ready for answers, but they had better come quickly."

Then I noticed an old, crumpled check lying on my table, but didn't attach any significance to it. As I was leaving the café after paying my own check, the waiter ran after me, saying that I had left something behind. It was the crumpled check, which turned out to be from a nearby bookshop. But still I wasn't particularly interested in it. (As I said, in those days I lacked experience in reading the signs).

Shortly afterwards, a passerby stopped me and asked for directions to a street that I didn't know. Barely two steps later, I realized I *had* seen the street name before – in the address of the bookshop on the crumpled check. Now that my curiosity had (finally) been aroused, I went there. It was a strange shop, with tubular bells in the window, and small clouds of smoke from incense sticks wafted towards me when I entered. It was one of the first esoteric bookshops in Munich. Until then I had had no idea that such a thing existed. Later it was to become my preferred bookshop.

Doubtfully I walked past the bookshelves. On the books, I read the names of authors that I'd never heard of before. I had no idea which book to buy, or indeed why I had found myself in this bookshop in the first place. Then a woman with close-cropped hair and almost ridiculously colorful cotton trousers turned round and said to me, "You must absolutely read that book – it's fantastic." With a knowing smile she indicated a book on the shelf.

More out of politeness than out of real interest, I actually bought it. This book turned my life upside down. It was *Das Handbuch zum höheren Bewusstsein* (the German translation of *Handbook to Higher Consciousness*) by Ken Keyes. It contained all the answers to my questions. Thanks to this book I suddenly realized the meaning of my doings.

But had this really been something along the lines of *successful wishing*, and had a higher order indeed led me to this book that afternoon?

We know how the mind works. It constantly doubts and claims that it was all just a string of coincidences.

So, shortly afterwards, I wanted to have another go. I was in search of another book that would have at least the same profound impact on my life.

This time I was bolder and more forthright in the formulation of my wish. I wanted to hold the book in my hands that same day and I expected to be informed of its title.

Furthermore, this time I didn't want to make it that easy for fate. I didn't want to leave the house. I actually didn't feel the slightest urge.

An hour later, my agent phoned me. She wanted to know whether I had finally read the script of the new episode of *Tatort* (*Crime Scene,* a German TV series). Of course not – I hadn't even received it yet. She was appalled. I should have read that script ages ago. It would be the role of my life. I was to come over to her office immediately and collect it.

On my way home, I suddenly recalled my wish. In the general commotion, I had completely forgotten it. And, by the look of things, the Universe had forgotten me, too. Where was my book, then?

Later that afternoon I went for a walk in Leopoldstraße, Munich (Leopold Street). Of course, I was alert and attentive. Perhaps someone would give me a hint again. Or I would catch a sentence somewhere containing the name of the book.

Nothing of that kind happened, however. I sat down on a street bench and read my script. Then I noticed a little boy who was standing in front of a shop and crying because he couldn't open the door. So I went and helped him. It was a bookshop and, barely three steps away from the cashier's desk, a small shock hit me. A book was staring at me and it was called *Mastery of Life* – a book that was to accompany me for over a year. It was as if Ron Smotherton had written it exclusively for me.

Hadn't my agent said that I should read the script, that it would be the role of my life?

The Universe always delivers. When we aren't sufficiently tuned in to our intuition, the Universe carries our 'parcel' after us until we cannot evade receiving it. If, however, we want to receive the delivery as soon as possible, it is imperative that we remain alert.

"Imagination is more important than knowledge. For knowledge is limited to all we now know and understand, while imagination embraces the entire world, and all there ever will be to know and understand."

Albert Einstein

The **Desire Code**:

Key 7 – Discover your true great wishes

Wishes are as diverse as individuals' personalities.

One person would like to learn to dance and never had the time, or had two left feet, another is looking for true friends, because their absence in his life is making itself more and more strongly felt, and the third is longing for the ideal partner.

Besides, no wish is greater or smaller, more important or more reprehensible than another. It also doesn't matter whether the wishes are sensible, in the sense that they appear logical to the mind. Each wish simply indicates the lack that we are feeling in certain areas of our life.

We have already learned that we have all our wishes fulfilled. The fundamental question is whether the fulfillment of our wish would also remedy our lack. Or would the lack soon make itself felt in another place? The real question is, therefore: "What is this lack in our life calling our attention to?"

What we are wishing for is quite simply change. There is something in our life that we don't like, and we don't know how to change it by 'normal' means. But often we don't know what it will really be like when the wish comes true. Will our life indeed improve?

What wishes are right for me?

That is the fundamental question. It makes no sense anyway to wish for something that doesn't harmonize with who we are. Yet most of us do just that. Often we wish for something only because others are wishing for it too, or already possess it. Often we chase an ideal that isn't ours at all.

But just because others think something's 'great', it by no means has to be right for us. And what are we to do when the longed-for situation materializes? That is to say, when wishes manifest that aren't appropriate for us at all?

Before we wish for something, we should be genuinely clear about what we actually need for our life. Will having something really make us better, more accepted, more lovable or happier?

The manifestation of many a wish can also put us under enormous pressure. Our dream job perhaps demands far more of us than we can handle, our wish to have a child may come true much too soon, or we may lose friends as a result of our desired change of residence.

Wishes that come true
always change us.

But are we really prepared for the changes and their con-sequences? That wonderful love affair that we so longed for may touch on our fear of falling short or of losing something we have long desired. Perhaps we won't have the courage to drive that large car, and because of its im-pressive size we'll never manage to find a parking space. Or we won't be able to handle the fame we desired and all the attention that comes with it.

Wishes that are fulfilled do not always bring us real happiness. Before tackling our major wishes, we should therefore be aware of what we are really expecting from their manifestation.

Every successful wish also changes our life circumstanc-es. For this reason we should scrutinize whether we are truly prepared for the change. Perhaps our desires lead in a certain direction, but we are not capable of actually fulfilling the new role at all yet.

Wishing for money

Coming by a lot of money may mean giving up our familiar surroundings, because we can now afford a house. Perhaps we will also lose our job, simply because we no longer need it and we don't see a deeper meaning in our work. We can now spend the whole day doing what we like, but do we really have the desire to do so? Maybe we'll miss our old apartment, our neighbors, our colleagues.

There is nothing wrong with wishing for a lot of money, but we should simply be aware that every wish has consequences. Perhaps it is therefore more crucial to consider the living conditions that we would like to create – because money alone is no guarantee of happiness. Many lottery winners become destitute and unhappier than ever just a few years after becoming millionaires overnight.

For that reason, Michaela and I have made a little deal with the Universe.

Our deal with the Universe

After winning two cars within the space of one year, we were deeply impressed by our *successful wishing*. But why should we always have to submit individual orders? Wouldn't it be possible to sign up for a standing subscription?

Immediately after winning the cars, Michaela and I had wished that we would never have to worry about money again. Money was to simply be there – not in excessive amounts, so that we would continue to derive sufficient joy and motivation from our work, but there should not be too little of it either.

In all events, it should always be present in our lives in such abundance that we would be able to realize our desires. It was like a deal with the Universe. We would do what the flow of time apparently wanted from us, and the Universe would continue to ensure that money regularly came in.

> Possessions should serve us,
> and not the other way round.

Since that day, the question of money has never arisen for us again. Money simply comes into our lives – sometimes in a totally unexpected way.

When you start wishing, one thing soon becomes clear: you don't become wealthy by working hard. You become wealthy by wishing for wealth and inviting it into your life. Only when you are convinced that you are entitled to it are you truly open and ready to receive the wished-for delivery.

But money is just one aspect of prosperity. True wealth encompasses considerably more. In order to be really happy, we should take the following aspects into account when wishing:

- health
- a wonderful relationship
- a fulfilling profession
- true friends

- enough time for ourselves and others

- inner peace and serenity

This list could be extended indefinitely. The important thing is to know that true wealth consists of more than just money. However, money, the 'filthy lucre', is an altogether desirable ingredient for more joy and inner freedom in life.

The dreamt-of relationship

It's probably the greatest wish of human beings: to find someone who will go through thick and thin with us, who understands us, with whom we feel loved and accepted. The wish for a partner is probably the one with the most profound impact on our lives. Especially when wishing for a partner, it is important to ask ourselves: "What do I really want?" That is, what characteristics should this person have?

In the well-known quote from his poem *Song of the Bell*, Friedrich Schiller (1759-1805) offers us the following sound advice:

> Whoe'er would form eternal bonds
> Should weigh if heart to heart responds.
> Folly is short – repentance long.

For the present-day wishing context, we could paraphrase this as:

> Consider carefully what you are really wishing
> for – because it will come true.

Of equal importance, though, is to examine your motives. "*Why* do I want a partner? What do I want him or her to add to my life?" It's often the case that what I want to receive from the other person is in reality missing inside me.

For example, if my wish runs, "I want someone who loves me unconditionally," then that in fact means "I'm not loved. I'm not lovable. I don't love myself." Many people are therefore in search of a partner who will love them unconditionally solely because they don't love themselves.

However, the actual starting point for the wish should be: "I'm lovable, just as I am. I accept all my flaws and shortcomings, and accept myself as I am now, just the same. I am unique and beautiful, and every day I come closer to my love for myself. Through my love for myself, I attract people who view me through the same eyes as I view myself. I am open and ready to allow my love for myself and the love of another person. I shall no longer give power to my obstacles and mental blockages, and the love inside me can flow freely. I am open and ready to allow love to manifest in my life."

If I were to just wish for someone who loves me without accepting myself, then I wouldn't be able to accept that other person's love for me either. It's only through my inner readiness that I can allow everything that I need. Then I, in fact, no longer have to search at all; I am found. For when we are truly ready, whatever we really need will find us.

There are, nevertheless, certain wishes that don't work out at all.

For example, wishes may not force other people to do something against their will. We can therefore not cause them to fall in love with us, or to do something very specific for us.

> Free will stands above everything,
> including any wish.

That is just as well, because otherwise anyone could wish something of us and we would suddenly have to perform actions that do not appeal to us in the least.

But how do I find the person who loves me, then?

Successful wishing will in any case not attract a specific person of my own choosing, as imagined by my mind, to commit to a relationship with me. However, when by wishing I invite a person into my life who resonates with me and of course returns my love, I am sure to get a partner who matches me and is appropriate for me.

Ordering the right partner

At my seminars on happy relationships, I always get the same question: "How do I meet the right partner and draw this person into my life?"

This is basically quite simple. This is so simple, actually, that for most of us it is incredibly difficult. Strictly speaking, we have to undertake far less action than we think. We simply have to stop our frantic and panic-stricken searching – because the frantic and panic-stricken searching only shows that we don't really trust the whole business. Deep down inside, we are usually convinced by then that we won't find anyone anymore. At least not Mr. or Ms. Right.

Searching is the opposite of finding.

In order to find, all we have to do is open our eyes and hearts, and be receptive.

> *Successful wishing* means being ready
> to allow all the miracles into our lives.

Searching prevents us from allowing. As long as we are searching, we are bound to a very specific object or goal – to the projection of an image that we have created in our limited consciousness and that we are now constantly looking out for. In our imagination, it will always be someone who is flawless. Of course, that is, after all, purely wishful thinking, without blemishes or dark sides. Such a person doesn't exist. Such a person exists only in our fantasy, which we can switch on and off at any time, or modify as we please.

However, we are looking for a person who is a good match for us. He or she will therefore have the same dark sides as we do. Strictly speaking, we are looking for ourselves, since we are ultimately seeking our own reflection in our beloved partner. He or she should be similar to us. He or she should evolve together with us and view the world from a similar perspective. He or she should think the same way about the most fundamental things in life – about faithfulness, family, love, God and how to deal with life's challenges.

Our imagination doesn't help us along in this respect. Nor does our incessant searching, which tends to prevent us from finding true love rather than allow us to experience it.

Before dispatching such a serious wish, we should be clear about what we really want.

To get this straight once again: the order itself is not difficult, but it has a major impact on our lives. In other words, it is very important to us. Any mistakes that we make when filling in our wish order form will therefore have far-reaching consequences.

And yet, despite its considerable significance, we often don't really have any idea of what our wish for the 'right' partner should look like. Although we think we know perfectly well what partner would be good for us, we in fact don't have the slightest clue. We don't want to spend a long time thinking about it, either; we simply want that partner. Behind this wish, however, there often lurks quite a different wish. We don't want to be alone anymore.

So, before placing our order, we should be clear about the kind of partner we want to have at our side in life.

Helpful in this respect is the list which I describe in detail in another of my books and briefly summarize here. This list clarifies for us pretty quickly what we expect from a relationship, what we are willing to contribute to it ourselves and, accordingly, what kind of partner is the best match for us. During my seminars and individual coaching sessions we very often work with this list. It is fast, effective and produces remarkable clarity.

If we want the 'right' partner, then, we must first be clear about what the Universe should search for on our behalf. This is how the list came into being. I developed it when – after many trials and tribulations and countless unsuccessful attempts – I finally wanted to find the right partner to share my future with.

At the time I had secluded myself for a while in order to figure out what partner would be a really good match for me.

To get clear about that, I tinkered with various tools and possibilities, always exploring the same question: "How can I best identify who would be a really good match for me?"

Then I hit on the idea of drawing up a list. In a nutshell, this is what I did:

I divided a large sheet of paper into two columns. In the first column I listed all the things that I expected from my future relationship. This column was filled fairly quickly and was quite extensive. All my wishes and longings came together there.

In the second column I wrote down all the things that I was willing to contribute to the relationship. And – lo and behold – this column was significantly shorter.

However, what I cannot bring to the table in a relationship, I will not find in it either. I was therefore quite obviously looking for a partner with whom I could work on developing all the things missing from the second column of my list.

As I got increasingly clear about what I expected my future partner to be like, I wrote everything down on a separate sheet of paper and laid it in a place of dignity.

The miraculous way in which this wish was fulfilled astonishes me to this day.

How I attracted the right partner into my life

I spent at least several weeks thinking over my wish for a partner and elaborating on it on the basis of my list.

Only when I was really absolutely certain about the person who would be the best match for me, did I hand over my wish list to the Universe.

Because one thing was clear to me: my wish would be fulfilled.

To be fair, however, I didn't exactly make it easy for the Universe to fulfill my wish. At this time I was leading a completely secluded life, spending most of the time at home for several months on end. Except for two hours on stage every evening at the Kurfürstendamm Theater, and one dinner in a wider social circle, at the gentle insistence of my colleagues (they feared it wasn't good for me to be alone in my apartment all the time), I lived in solitude.

How on earth was the Universe going to manifest my wish under these circumstances?

A few weeks later, the phone rang. The caller was a woman with whom I had spoken a few weeks previously at the aforementioned dinner. I couldn't remember her too well, though. I recalled her as being blonde and slender, and wearing thick glasses. But on the phone we hit it off so well that we spent four hours talking, and another seven hours the next day.

And as we couldn't meet in person – she was appearing in a play in Bremen, while I was on stage in Berlin – we phoned for seven hours the day after that as well. We felt such a deep mutual understanding about so many things that the following night – after another eight hours on the phone – we agreed to go on vacation together.

The sense of connection we felt was so intense that a day later we even decided – by phone – to move in together. Michaela, showing herself capable of true abandon, immediately gave both her employer and her landlord notice that she was leaving. A day later – and without actually having seen each other – we decided to get married.

But so soon? Even though – *apparently* – we hardly knew each other, at the same time it felt like we'd known each other our whole lives.

We were intimately acquainted with every millimeter of each other's souls. We had told each other everything about ourselves. There were no secrets. Even things that we had never told anyone else, we knew about each other. We had revealed ourselves. We had, so to speak, laid out all that we had to offer each other on a vendor's tray and bared our souls without reservation. We both knew that we belonged together.

All my friends considered me totally mad. They thought I was now completely mentally deranged. They tried to get me to change my mind: "You don't even know how she smells, how she tastes or whether you're compatible physically."

But I knew that if I didn't give myself the chance to live with my true great love, I would regret it for the rest of my life. Whenever I would be going through a rough relationship patch with someone else, I would always think of this unique opportunity. And of my own failure and fickleness.

On the other hand, what risk was I actually running? Should it turn out that Michaela and I would not harmonize physically, then we still had a chance to become the best of friends. For we were already soul mates.

She thought the way I did; she saw the world through the same eyes; she had the same hopes and desires, and was just as willing as I was to work on herself, so that we could mutually resolve all the flaws in our respective personalities.

And when, six weeks later and after many more long phone conversations, I turned up in front of her house with a moving van and saw her properly for the first time, I was overjoyed. My first thought was: you lucky devil. Michaela was the most beautiful woman I could ever have imagined.

The most astonishing thing was, though, that when I later dug up my list and reviewed my order from the Universe, Michaela fitted the bill precisely, right down to the tiniest detail.

Of course, we always also receive a few extras, things and characteristics that we hadn't included on our wish list. After all, we can't think of everything. But everything that I had written on my piece of paper was fulfilled.

Coincidence? Those who still believe in that should continue to leave their lives to chance and struggle on. It's far easier to harness *successful wishing* and to take our lives into our own hands.

As can be seen clearly from my example, however, we should not have any expectations about the way in which the delivery should occur.

It is solely a matter of being ready. Our new partner can bowl us over, cause an accident or sue us. Who says that our first encounter has to be positive? It will always attract our entire attention.

Many happy marriages started with the couple loathing each other, but – strangely enough – not being dissimilar to each other either. Of course, it's equally possible that the relationship will evolve perfectly romantically from the outset, and that both will immediately know that the other is their partner for life.

The only important thing is to simply have no fixed opinions and ideas about how the manifestation of the wish must unfold. Otherwise the Universe might be in the act of delivering our order, and we will totally miss out on the delivery by being inwardly absent.

People often ask me whether Michaela had likewise sent out a wish for the right partner into the ether at the same time as I had done.

No, she hadn't. But she was open and willing to commit to a relationship.

Of course she might have said no, but then that would have been one of the most peculiar deliveries of my life. "This would be the most wonderful woman, who is a perfect match for you, but she doesn't want you at all."

Well, that is just not the way the Universe delivers. Michaela was open and ready, and I was in search of the ideal partner, who would of course be open and ready for a loving relationship.

Apart from that, you can indeed put on your list anything that occurs to you – including appearance, figure and character traits. But be aware that this does not guarantee that you will be happy with such a partner; you may well be stifling your wishes.

For example, suppose that your ideal partner is sporty and athletic, and of course good-looking. In that case we have to assume that this future partner is also fond of sports activities and would like to pursue these together with us. Is that what we really want?

Or suppose that we wish for a partner who's a rocket between the sheets and has an insatiable lust – every man's dream. But when this dream becomes reality, it can soon turn into a nightmare. What if, after a month, you want sex less often than she does, or you can't keep pace with her, or you want to pursue other interests as well?

Or you fear that she'll dump you if you don't live up to her expectations in bed? Or you're afraid that you can't satisfy her?

If we wish for a gorgeous partner, while considering ourselves less good-looking, then we might soon feel inferior.

Formulating our wishes solely from our present state of lack can therefore be pretty dangerous. The wish will come true. But there's no guarantee that the manifestation is in our best interests.

Especially when wishing for a partner, therefore, we should think very carefully about the kind of partner we would like to attract.

"A dream is a wish the heart makes."
Walt Disney

Does life become happier?

Does *successful wishing* make us happier? Yes, definitely – but in unexpected ways.

Happiness is an inner attitude and has very little to do with outer reality. If we aren't happy without money or a partner, then having these in our lives will not make us happy.

After all, don't we all know people who 'have it all' – money, a partner, fame – and yet are permanently bad-tempered or unhappy?

If we want to experience happiness, we will not do so through outside influences.

This is because happiness always originates inside ourselves. We experience happiness when we send out happiness. And it doesn't matter whether we are living in a villa or in a 300-square-foot apartment – we can be equally happy or unhappy in both.

Happiness comes from an inner serenity. Happiness always arises when we want to share something with others.

Happiness is a state in which we find ourselves, with or without a partner, with or without money, with or without a house and status. Many people, however, believe that they can be happy only if they possess something specific. And it's precisely that little word 'if' that holds our happiness hostage – forever.

We're absolutely not interested in figuring out why we are in our current situation – we simply want to get out of it. However, given that this undesirable situation is the result of certain circumstances, namely our own subconscious wishes and beliefs that we refuse to embrace, we will continue to think and act in similar ways even if our outer circumstances change.

We always take ourselves with us.

Thus we are also our own companions on the path to our alleged happiness, which of course always lies elsewhere. And that's why we will remain unhappy even when we do attain the situation that is supposed to make us happy. There will always be something missing in our lives and preventing us from experiencing true happiness.

Many years ago, I seemingly had it all. Money, status, professional success, women and health. And yet I wasn't happy. I felt empty and driven. I was still convinced that everyone else was better off than I was. I was convinced that I needed to have more in order to come closer to happiness. In other words, I needed to become even more successful, accumulate even more possessions and go to bed with even more women, and then that feeling of deep bliss would set in.

And it was precisely this belief that did not allow me to be happy. Precisely this belief in my lack that led me to experience it more than ever. Without knowing it, I was shifting my happiness into the future. My belief in lack drowned out all my other wishes.

So strongly did I believe in this lack, which seemingly impeded my happiness, that even when the first wishes manifested, they weren't the right ones for me, or they manifested far too late. For this reason, I couldn't receive anything that the Universe delivered on my orders – absolutely nothing whatsoever – with joy and gratitude. At the same time, I was convinced that other people had had far better wishes fulfilled.

I was in search of happiness, yet the more I looked for it outside myself, the more I lost sight of it. My subconscious wish at the time ran, "I'm not happy. My happiness lies in the future. I need even more in order to be happy."

Hence I was quite concretely ordering: "Never experiencing happiness in the present." My basic attitude was one of unhappiness. And even the fulfillment of my wishes, whether a few or many, could not alter that.

Only when I gave up and let go of the compelling notion of attaining happiness through others did I start to find deep contentment and love.

Ultimately, my search was always triggered by the same thing: my longing for love and security. Because I lacked these, I hoped to obtain them through outside influences.

However, when we do not feel love and security inside ourselves, no person on this earth can give them to us.

That means, as much as I regret to say, that the fulfillment of all of our wishes does not alter our basic attitude to happiness. If we aren't happy now, then we won't become happy as a result of outside influences – even though we sometimes believe we will. The happiness we experience in such cases is short-lived, because it doesn't correspond with our very nature.

Has *successful wishing* made me happier?

Yes, absolutely! Not so much because everything I wish for nowadays materializes in my life, but rather because I live more consciously and trust that I am being guided.

I have repeatedly been allowed to experience the fact that my wishes manifest if I want them to. That very fact has taught me that I do not need to struggle along on my own on this earth. Even in the quietest and loneliest moments I am fulfilled and happy. Whether I'm completely withdrawn or out walking, I am connected. And brimming with gratitude.

> Joining forces with the Universe is considerably easier than struggling along on your own.

The Desire Code changed my whole world: how I experience and perceive things; my relationship and my love for myself.

Every day I come closer to myself – with the help of *successful wishing*.

With each subsequent wish that was fulfilled, I better understood what was truly significant in my life. When we can achieve everything, when we can have anything, we start to examine our real wishes more closely.

Ultimately, it is always only love that we are seeking.

Ultimately, it is always only love that makes us happy.

Love for ourselves – and for others.

ABOUT THE AUTHOR

A bestselling author with more than 60 titles published in 11 countries and sales of more than 3 million, Pierre Franckh lectures around the world and hosts sold-out seminars. He is also a motivational coach and inspirational speaker with numerous clients in the business world, as well as doctors, psychologists, and complementary health professionals. Countless people have successfully changed their lives as a result of his work. He lives in Munich and London with his wife, Michaela and daughter, Julia.

www.pierre-franckh.com

www.thedesirecodebook.com

20822480R00091

Made in the USA
San Bernardino, CA
30 December 2018